# ACCOUNTING PRINCIPLES

# FIFTH CANADIAN EDITION

# ACCOUNTING PRINCIPLES

## WORKING PAPERS
Part 1
Chapters 1-7

- **Jerry J. Weygandt** Ph.D., C.P.A.
  Arthur Andersen Alumni Professor of Accounting
  University of Wisconsin—Madison

- **Donald E. Kieso** Ph.D., C.P.A.
  KPMG Peat Marwick Emeritus Professor of Accountancy
  Northern Illinois University

- **Paul D. Kimmel** Ph.D., C.P.A.
  University of Wisconsin—Milwaukee

- **Barbara Trenholm** M.B.A., F.C.A.
  University of New Brunswick—Fredericton

- **Valerie Kinnear** M.Sc. (Bus. Admin.), C.A.
  Mount Royal University

PREPARED BY BARBARA TRENHOLM

John Wiley & Sons Canada, Ltd.

Copyright © 2010 by John Wiley & Sons Canada, Ltd

Copyright © 2009 by John Wiley & Sons Inc. All rights reserved. No part of this work covered by the copyrights herein may be reproduced or used in any form or by any means—graphic, electronic, or mechanical—without the prior written permission of the publisher.

Any request for photocopying, recording, taping or inclusion in information storage and retrieval systems of any part of this book shall be directed in writing to The Canadian Copyright Licensing Agency (Access Copyright). For an Access Copyright Licence, visit www.accesscopyright.ca or toll-free, 1-800-893-5777.

Care has been taken to trace ownership of copyright material contained in this text. The publishers will gladly receive any information that will enable them to rectify any erroneous reference or credit line in subsequent editions.

**Library and Archives Canada Cataloguing in Publication**

Trenholm, Barbara A.
    Accounting principles, fifth Canadian edition, Jerry J. Weygandt ....
Working papers / prepared by Barbara Trenholm.

ISBN 978-0-470-67757-5 (pt. 1).--ISBN 978-0-470-67919-7 (pt. 2)

    1. Accounting--Problems, exercises, etc. I. Title.

HF5636.A33 2009a Suppl. 3      657'.044      C2010-900745-X

**Production Credits**

Acquisitions Editor: Zoë Craig
Vice President & Publisher: Veronica Visentin
Vice President, Publishing Services: Karen Bryan
Creative Director, Publishing Services: Ian Koo
Marketing Manager: Aida Krneta
Editorial Manager: Karen Staudinger
Editorial Assistant: Laura Hwee
Cover Design: Natalia Burobina
Printing & Binding: EPAC Book Services

Printed and bound in the United States
1 2 3 4 5 EPAC 14 13 112 11 10

John Wiley & Sons Canada, Ltd.
6045 Freemont Blvd.
Mississauga, Ontario L5R 4J3
Visit our website at: www.wiley.ca

# CONTENTS PART 1

CHAPTER 1    ACCOUNTING IN ACTION
CHAPTER 2    THE RECORDING PROCESS
CHAPTER 3    ADJUSTING THE ACCOUNTS
CHAPTER 4    COMPLETION OF THE ACCOUNTING CYCLE
CHAPTER 5    ACCOUNTING FOR MERCHANDISING OPERATIONS
CHAPTER 6    INVENTORY COSTING
CHAPTER 7    INTERNAL CONTROL AND CASH

                BLANK FINANCIAL ACCOUNTING FORMS

Name             Brief Exercises 1-1 to 1-5

**BE1-1**

| User | (a) Kind of Decision | (b) Internal or External User |
|---|---|---|
| Owner | | |
| Marketing manager | | |
| Creditor | | |
| Chief financial officer | | |
| Labour union | | |

**BE1-2**

1.
2.
3.
4.
5.

**BE1-3**

(a)
(b)
(c)

**BE1-4**

(a)
(b)
(c)
(d)
(e)
(f)

**BE1-5**

(a)
(b)
(c)
(d)
(e)

Name  Brief Exercises 1-6 to 1-9

**BE1-6**

**BE1-7**

**BE1-8**

**BE1-9**

| | |
|---|---|
| (a) | (g) |
| (b) | (h) |
| (c) | (i) |
| (d) | (j) |
| (e) | (k) |
| (f) | (l) |

# Brief Exercises 1-10 to 1-13

## BE1-10

| Trans. | Assets | Liabilities | Owner's Equity Capital | Drawings | Revenues | Expenses |
|---|---|---|---|---|---|---|
| 1. | +$250 | +$250 | NE | NE | NE | NE |
| 2. | | | | | | |
| 3. | | | | | | |
| 4. | | | | | | |
| 5. | | | | | | |
| 6. | | | | | | |
| 7. | | | | | | |
| 8. | | | | | | |

## BE1-11

| | |
|---|---|
| (a) | Cost incurred for advertising |
| (b) | Commission earnings |
| (c) | Equipment received from company owner |
| (d) | Amounts paid to employees |
| (e) | Cash paid to purchase equipment |
| (f) | Services performed on account |
| (g) | Rent received |
| (h) | Utilities incurred |
| (i) | Cash distributed to company owner |
| (j) | Collection of an account receivable |

## BE1-12

| | | (a) | (b) |
|---|---|---|---|
| 1. | Accounts receivable | A | BS |
| 2. | Wages payable | | |
| 3. | Wage expense | | |
| 4. | Office supplies | | |
| 5. | Supplies expense | | |
| 6. | K. Sen, capital (opening) | | |
| 7. | K. Sen, capital (closing) | | |
| 8. | Service revenue | | |
| 9. | Equipment | | |
| 10. | Note payable | | |
| 11. | Cash | | |
| 12. | K. Sen, drawings | | |

## BE1-13

Name  Brief Exercises 1-14 to 1-15

**BE1-14**

| | |
|---|---|
| (a) | (g) |
| (b) | (h) |
| (c) | (i) |
| (d) | (j) |
| (e) | (k) |
| (f) | |

**BE1-15**

**BE1-16**

PORTAGE COMPANY
Income Statement
Month Ended August 31, 2011

|  |  |  |
|---|---|---|
|  |  |  |
|  |  |  |
|  |  |  |
|  |  |  |
|  |  |  |
|  |  |  |
|  |  |  |
|  |  |  |

**BE1-17**

PORTAGE COMPANY
Statement of Owner's Equity
Month Ended August 31, 2011

|  |  |  |
|---|---|---|
|  |  |  |
|  |  |  |
|  |  |  |
|  |  |  |
|  |  |  |
|  |  |  |
|  |  |  |
|  |  |  |

**BE1-18**

PORTAGE COMPANY
Balance Sheet
August 31, 2011

|  |  |  |
|---|---|---|
|  |  |  |
|  |  |  |
|  |  |  |
|  |  |  |
|  |  |  |
|  |  |  |
|  |  |  |
|  |  |  |
|  |  |  |
|  |  |  |
|  |  |  |
|  |  |  |
|  |  |  |
|  |  |  |

**E1-1**

**E1-2**

**E1-3**

(a)
(b)
(c)
(d)
(e)
(f)
(g)
(h)
(i)
(j)

**E1-4**

|    | Proprietorship | Partnership | Corporation |
|----|----------------|-------------|-------------|
| 1. |                |             |             |
| 2. |                |             |             |
| 3. |                |             |             |
| 4. |                |             |             |
| 5. |                |             |             |
| 6. |                |             |             |
| 7. |                |             |             |
| 8. |                |             |             |
| 9. |                |             |             |

**E1-5**

(a)
- Accounts payable
- Accounts receivable
- Cash
- Inventories
- Investments
- Land, buildings, and equipment
- Notes payable
- Other assets
- Other liabilities
- Retained earnings
- Share capital

(b)

Name                                                                                           Exercise 1-6

**E1-7**

**E1-8**

Name _____

Exercises 1-9 to 1-10

| E1-9 Trans. | Assets | = | Liabilities | + | Owner's Equity |
|---|---|---|---|---|---|
| 1. | | | | | |
| 2. | | | | | |
| 3. | | | | | |
| 4. | | | | | |
| 5. | | | | | |
| 6. | | | | | |
| 7. | | | | | |
| 8. | | | | | |
| 9. | | | | | |
| 10. | | | | | |
| Total | | | | | |

| E1-10 Trans. | Assets | = | Liabilities | + | Owner's Equity |
|---|---|---|---|---|---|
| 1. | | | | | |
| 2. | | | | | |
| 3. | | | | | |
| 4. | | | | | |
| 5. | | | | | |
| 6. | | | | | |
| 7. | | | | | |
| 8. | | | | | |
| 9. | | | | | |
| 10. | | | | | |
| Total | | | | | |

Name  Exercises 1-11 to 1-12

**E1-11 (a)**
1.
2.
3.
4.
5.
6.
7.
8.
9.
10.

(b)

(c)

| E1-12 | | (a) | (b) |
|---|---|---|---|
| 1. | Accounts payable | L | BS |
| 2. | Accounts receivable | | |
| 3. | Cash | | |
| 4. | Dental equipment | | |
| 5. | Furniture and fixtures | | |
| 6. | Interest payable | | |
| 7. | Interest revenue | | |
| 8. | Interest expense | | |
| 9. | Investment by the owner | | |
| 10. | Orthodontist fees earned | | |
| 11. | P. Zizler, capital (opening balance) | | |
| 12. | P. Zizler, drawings | | |
| 13. | Salaries expense | | |
| 14. | Supplies | | |
| 15. | Supplies expense | | |

Name  Exercise 1-13

BNITA & CO.
Income Statement
Month Ended August 31, 2011

BNITA & CO.
Statement of Owner's Equity
Month Ended August 31, 2011

BNITA & CO.
Balance Sheet
August 31, 2011

**E1-14**

**E1-15**

Name  Exercise 1-16

**(a) and (b)**

**(c)**

Name                                                                 Problem 1-1A

*Taking It Further*

Name  Problem 1-2A

**Taking It Further**

Name　　　　　　　　　　　　　　　　　　　　　　　　　　　　　　　　Problem 1-3A

*Taking It Further*

Problem 1-4A

**Problem 1-4A Concluded**

*Taking It Further*

Problem 1-5A

| (a) Date | Assets | | | = | Liabilities | | + | Owner's Equity | | |
|---|---|---|---|---|---|---|---|---|---|---|
| Apr. 1 | | | | | | | | | | |
| 2 | | | | | | | | | | |
| 2 | | | | | | | | | | |
| 7 | | | | | | | | | | |
| 8 | | | | | | | | | | |
| 11 | | | | | | | | | | |
| 17 | | | | | | | | | | |
| 25 | | | | | | | | | | |
| 30 | | | | | | | | | | |
| 30 | | | | | | | | | | |
| 30 | | | | | | | | | | |
| Total | | | | | | | | | | |

**Name** Problem 1-5A Concluded

(b)

**Taking It Further**

Name                                                                                                                    Problem 1-6A

|     | (a) | (b) |                          |         |
|-----|-----|-----|--------------------------|---------|
| 1.  | L   | BS  | Accounts payable         | $ 1,197 |
| 2.  |     |     | Accounts receivable      | 547     |
| 3.  |     |     | Aircraft fuel expense    | 432     |
| 4.  |     |     | Airport fee expense      | 309     |
| 5.  |     |     | Interest expense         | 161     |
| 6.  |     |     | Cash                     | 632     |
| 7.  |     |     | C.Chung, capital, January 1 | 1,160 |
| 8.  |     |     | C.Chung, drawings        | 14      |
| 9.  |     |     | Interest expense         | 75      |
| 10. |     |     | Maintenance expense      | 78      |
| 11. |     |     | Notes payable            | 2,536   |
| 12. |     |     | Other assets             | 1,270   |
| 13. |     |     | Other expenses           | 650     |
| 14. |     |     | Other liabilities        | 1,436   |
| 15. |     |     | Other revenue            | 230     |
| 16. |     |     | Passenger revenues       | 1,681   |
| 17. |     |     | Property and equipment   | 3,561   |
| 18. |     |     | Salaries expense         | 596     |
| 19. |     |     | Spare parts and supplies | 237     |

(c)

Taking It Further

# Problem 1-7A

## (a)

| Trans | Assets | = | Liabilities | + | Owner's Equity |
|---|---|---|---|---|---|
| 1. | | | | | |
| 2. | | | | | |
| 3. | | | | | |
| 4. | | | | | |
| 5. | | | | | |
| 6. | | | | | |
| 7. | | | | | |
| 8. | | | | | |
| 9. | | | | | |
| 10. | | | | | |
| 11. | | | | | |
| 12. | | | | | |
| Total | | | | | |

(b)

Name **Problem 1-7A Concluded**

(c)

*Taking It Further*

Name  
Problem 1-8A

(a)

| Date | Assets | | | | | = | Liabilities | | + | Owner's Equity | | | |
|------|--------|--|--|--|--|---|-------------|--|---|----------------|--|--|--|
|      | Cash | Accounts Receivable | Supplies | Office Equipment | | = | Notes Payable | Accounts Payable | + | T. Tiberio, Capital | T. Tiberio, Drawings | Revenues | Expenses |
| Bal. | $4,000 | $1,900 | $500 | $5,000 | | = | | $5,500 | + | $5,900 | | | |
| Aug. 4 | | | | | | | | | | | | | |
| 5 | | | | | | | | | | | | | |
| 7 | | | | | | | | | | | | | |
| 12 | | | | | | | | | | | | | |
| 15 | | | | | | | | | | | | | |
| 18 | | | | | | | | | | | | | |
| 20 | | | | | | | | | | | | | |
| 26 | | | | | | | | | | | | | |
| 28 | | | | | | | | | | | | | |
| 29 | | | | | | | | | | | | | |
| 30 | | | | | | | | | | | | | |
| Total | | | | | | | | | | | | | |

(b)

Name                                                                                                    Problem 1-8A Concluded

**(b) (Concluded)**

*Taking It Further*

Problem 1-9A

Problem 1-9A Concluded

*Taking It Further*

**(a)**

(i)
(ii)
(iii)
(iv)
(v)
(vi)
(vii)
(viii)
(ix)
(x)

**(b)**

*Taking It Further*

Name	Problem 1-11A

(a)

(b)

**Problem 1-11A Concluded**

(b)

*Taking It Further*

Name:  Brief Exercises 2-1 to 2-2

**BE2-1**

| Accounts Receivable ||
|---|---|
| 8,000 | 5,210 |
| 6,340 | 2,750 |
|  | 2,390 |

| Accounts Payable ||
|---|---|
| 220 | 390 |
| 560 | 710 |
| 175 | 850 |
| 355 |  |

**BE2-2**

| | (a) Type of Account | (b) Financial Statement | (c) Normal Balance |
|---|---|---|---|
| 1. Accounts Receivable | | | |
| 2. Accounts Payable | | | |
| 3. Equipment | | | |
| 4. Rent Expense | | | |
| 5. B. Damji, Drawings | | | |
| 6. Supplies | | | |
| 7. Unearned Revenue | | | |
| 8. Cash | | | |
| 9. Service Revenue | | | |
| 10. Prepaid Insurance | | | |

*Accounting Principles, 5th Canadian Edition*

Name:            Brief Exercises 2-3 to 2-4

| BE2-3 | (a) Debit Effect | (b) Credit Effect | (c) Normal Balance |
|---|---|---|---|
| 1. Accounts Payable | | | |
| 2. Accounts Receivable | | | |
| 3. Cash | | | |
| 4. Office Equipment | | | |
| 5. J. Takamoto, Capital | | | |
| 6. J. Takamoto, Drawings | | | |
| 7. Notes Payable | | | |
| 8. Prepaid Rent | | | |
| 9. Insurance Expense | | | |
| 10. Salaries Expense | | | |
| 11. Service Revenue | | | |
| 12. Unearned Revenue | | | |

**BE2-4**

1.

2.

3.

4.

5.

6.

7.

8.

*Accounting Principles, 5th Canadian Edition*        Working Papers, Chapter 2

**Brief Exercises 2-5 to 2-6**

| BE2-5 | Account Debited | | | Account Credited | | |
|---|---|---|---|---|---|---|
| | (a) Specific Account | (b) Basic Type | Type Of Owner's Equity Account | (a) Specific Account | (b) Basic Type | Type Of Owner's Equity Account |
| 1. | | | | | | |
| 2. | | | | | | |
| 3. | | | | | | |
| 4. | | | | | | |
| 5. | | | | | | |
| 6. | | | | | | |
| 7. | | | | | | |
| 8. | | | | | | |

| BE2-6 | Account Debited | Account Credited |
|---|---|---|
| June 1 | | |
| 2 | | |
| 3 | | |
| 4 | | |
| 12 | | |
| 22 | | |
| 25 | | |
| 29 | | |

Name: Brief Exercises 2-7 to 2-8

| BE2-7 | | Account Debited | | | Account Credited | | |
|---|---|---|---|---|---|---|---|
| | (a) Basic Type | (b) Specific Account | (c) Effect | (a) Basic Type | (b) Specific Account | (c) Effect |
| Aug. 1 | Asset | Cash | +$17,000 | Owner's equity | J. Fischer, Capital | +$17,000 |
| 4 | | | | | | |
| 5 | | | | | | |
| 6 | | | | | | |
| 17 | | | | | | |
| 27 | | | | | | |
| 29 | | | | | | |

| BE2-8 | General Journal | | |
|---|---|---|---|
| Date | Account Titles and Explanation | Debit | Credit |
| June 1 | | | |
| 2 | | | |
| 3 | | | |
| 4 | | | |
| 12 | | | |
| 22 | | | |
| 25 | | | |
| 29 | | | |

*Accounting Principles, 5th Canadian Edition*

Brief Exercise 2-9

| Date | Account Titles and Explanation | Debit | Credit |
|------|-------------------------------|-------|--------|
|      |                               |       |        |

Name: _____                                               Brief Exercise 2-10

| Cash | J. Fischer, Capital |
|---|---|
| | |

| Accounts Receivable | J. Fischer, Drawings |
|---|---|
| | |

| Prepaid Rent | Service Revenue |
|---|---|
| | |

| Supplies | Salaries Expense |
|---|---|
| | |

| Accounts Payable | |
|---|---|
| | |

Name: _____                    Brief Exercises 2-11 to 2-12

**BE2-11**

|          Cash          |     Service Revenue     |
|------------------------|-------------------------|

|        Furniture       |     Accounts Payable    |
|------------------------|-------------------------|

|   Accounts Receivable  |     Salaries Expense    |
|------------------------|-------------------------|

**BE2-12**

PETTIPAS COMPANY
Trial Balance
April 30, 2011

|  | Debit | Credit |
|---|---|---|
|  |  |  |
|  |  |  |
|  |  |  |
|  |  |  |
|  |  |  |
|  |  |  |
|  |  |  |
|  |  |  |
|  |  |  |
|  |  |  |
|  |  |  |
|  |  |  |
|  |  |  |
|  |  |  |
|  |  |  |
|  |  |  |
|  |  |  |
|  |  |  |
|  |  |  |

*Accounting Principles, 5th Canadian Edition*                                *Working Papers, Chapter 2*

Brief Exercise 2-13

| | BOURQUE COMPANY | | |
|---|---|---|---|
| | Trial Balance--Revised (Optional) | | |
| | December-31-10 | | |
| | | Debit | Credit |
| | | | |
| | | | |
| | | | |
| | | | |
| | | | |
| | | | |
| | | | |
| | | | |
| | | | |
| | | | |
| | | | |
| | | | |
| | | | |
| | | | |
| | | | |
| | | | |

Name: _____                                    Exercises 2-1 to 2-2

| E2-1 |
|---|
| (a) |
| (b) |
| (c) |
| (d) |
| (e) |
| (f) |
| (g) |
| (h) |
| (i) |
| (j) |

| E2-2 Account | (1) Type of Account | (2) Financial Statement | (3) Normal Balance |
|---|---|---|---|
| 1. Cash | Asset | Balance sheet | Debit |
| 2. M. Kobayashi, Capital | | | |
| 3. Accounts Payable | | | |
| 4. Building | | | |
| 5. Consulting Fee Revenue | | | |
| 6. Insurance Expense | | | |
| 7. Interest Earned | | | |
| 8. Notes Receivable | | | |
| 9. Prepaid Insurance | | | |
| 10. Rent Expense | | | |
| 11. Supplies | | | |

*Accounting Principles, 5th Canadian Edition*                *Working Papers, Chapter 2*

Name:     Exercises 2-3 to 2-4

### E2-3

| Trans. | Account Debited | | | Account Credited | | |
|---|---|---|---|---|---|---|
| | (a) Basic Type | (b) Specific Account | (d) Effect | (a) Basic Type | (b) Specific Account | (d) Effect |
| Mar. 3 | Asset | Cash | +$10,000 | Owner's Equity | L. Visser, Capital | +$10,000 |
| 6 | | | | | | |
| 7 | | | | | | |
| 12 | | | | | | |
| 21 | | | | | | |
| 25 | | | | | | |
| 28 | | | | | | |
| 30 | | | | | | |
| 31 | | | | | | |

### E2-4 General Journal

| Date | Account Titles and Explanation | Debit | Credit |
|---|---|---|---|
| Mar. 3 | | | |
| | | | |
| | | | |
| 6 | | | |
| | | | |
| | | | |
| 7 | | | |
| | | | |
| | | | |
| 12 | | | |
| | | | |
| | | | |
| 21 | | | |
| | | | |
| | | | |
| 25 | | | |
| | | | |
| | | | |
| 28 | | | |
| | | | |
| | | | |
| 30 | | | |
| | | | |
| | | | |
| 31 | | | |
| | | | |
| | | | |

*Accounting Principles, 5th Canadian Edition*

Exercise 2-5

## General Journal

| Date | Account Titles and Explanation | Debit | Credit |
|------|-------------------------------|-------|--------|
|      |                               |       |        |

Name  Exercise 2-6

(a) and (b)

### General Journal

| Trans. | Account Titles and Explanation | Debit | Credit |
|---|---|---|---|
| | | | |

(c)

## E2-7

| Cash | S. Gardiner, Capital |
|---|---|
| Accounts Receivable | Fees Earned |
| Office Equipment | Salaries Expense |
| Note Payable | Advertising Expense |
| Accounts Payable | Telephone Expense |

## E2-8

Name:                                                                                  Exercise 2-9

(a) General Journal

| Date | Account Titles and Explanation | Debit | Credit |
|------|-------------------------------|-------|--------|
|      |                               |       |        |

*Accounting Principles, 5th Canadian Edition*                                    *Working Papers, Chapter 2*

**(a) (Continued)** General Journal

| Date | Account Titles and Explanation | Debit | Credit |
|------|-------------------------------|-------|--------|
|      |                               |       |        |

**(b)**

FORTIN CO.
Trial Balance
October 31, 2011

|   | Debit | Credit |
|---|-------|--------|
|   |       |        |

Name: _____                                                                 Exercise 2-10

**(a) and (b)**

|      Cash       |   Accounts Receivable   |      Supplies       |
|-----------------|-------------------------|---------------------|

|    Equipment    |     Notes Payable       |  Accounts Payable   |
|-----------------|-------------------------|---------------------|

| L. Meche, Capital | L. Meche, Drawings    | Medical Fee Revenue |
|-------------------|-----------------------|---------------------|

|  Rent Expense   |    Salaries Expense     |                     |
|-----------------|-------------------------|---------------------|

**(c)**

|  | Debit | Credit |
|--|-------|--------|
|  |       |        |
|  |       |        |
|  |       |        |
|  |       |        |
|  |       |        |
|  |       |        |
|  |       |        |
|  |       |        |
|  |       |        |
|  |       |        |
|  |       |        |
|  |       |        |
|  |       |        |

*Accounting Principles, 5th Canadian Edition*                    *Working Papers, Chapter*

Exercises 2-11 to 2-12

| E2-11 Error | (a) In Balance | (b) Difference | (c) Larger Column |
|---|---|---|---|
| 1. | No | $400 | Debit |
| 2. | | | |
| 3. | | | |
| 4. | | | |
| 5. | | | |
| 6. | | | |

E2-12

| | Debit | Credit |
|---|---|---|
| | | |

Exercise 2-13

**O'CALLAGHAN'S COUNSELLING SERVICES**
Income Statement
Year Ended July 31, 2011

**O'CALLAGHAN'S COUNSELLING SERVICES**
Statement of Owner's Equity
Year Ended July 31, 2011

**O'CALLAGHAN'S COUNSELLING SERVICES**
Balance Sheet
July 31, 2011

Problem 2-1A

| Account | (a) Type of Account | (b) Financial Statement | (c) Normal Balance | (d) Increase | (e) Decrease |
|---|---|---|---|---|---|
| Accounts Payable | Liability | Balance sheet | Credit | Credit | Debit |
| Accounts Receivable | | | | | |
| Building | | | | | |
| Cash | | | | | |
| Equipment | | | | | |
| Insurance Expense | | | | | |
| Interest Earned | | | | | |
| Land | | | | | |
| Legal Fees Earned | | | | | |
| M. Brock, Capital | | | | | |
| M. Brock, Drawings | | | | | |
| Notes Receivable | | | | | |
| Prepaid Insurance | | | | | |
| Rent Expense | | | | | |
| Rent Revenue | | | | | |
| Salaries Expense | | | | | |
| Salaries Payable | | | | | |
| Supplies | | | | | |
| Supplies Expense | | | | | |
| Unearned Legal Fees | | | | | |

*Taking It Further*

Accounting Principles, 5th Canadian Edition

Name:     Problem 2-2A

### (a)

| Trans-action | Account Debited | | | Account Credited | | |
|---|---|---|---|---|---|---|
| | (1) Basic Type | (2) Specific Account | (3) Effect | (1) Basic Type | (2) Specific Account | (3) Effect |
| Apr. 1 | Asset | Cash | +$13,500 | Owner's equity | J. Butterfield, Capital | +$13,500 |
| 2 | | | | | | |
| 2 | | | | | | |
| 3 | | | | | | |
| 7 | | | | | | |
| 8 | | | | | | |
| 10 | | | | | | |
| 25 | | | | | | |
| 27 | | | | | | |
| 28 | | | | | | |
| 30 | | | | | | |

### (b) General Journal

| Date | Account Titles and Explanation | Debit | Credit |
|---|---|---|---|
| | | | |

**Problem 2-2A Concluded**

(b)

## General Journal

| Date | Account Titles and Explanation | Debit | Credit |
|------|-------------------------------|-------|--------|
|      |                               |       |        |

**Taking It Further**

# General Journal

| Date | Account Titles and Explanation | Debit | Credit |
|------|-------------------------------|-------|--------|
|      |                               |       |        |

**Problem 2-3A Concluded**

(b) General Journal

| Date | Account Titles and Explanation | Debit | Credit |
|------|-------------------------------|-------|--------|
|      |                               |       |        |

*Taking It Further*

**Problem 2-4A**

## General Journal (a)

| Date | Account Titles and Explanation | Debit | Credit |
|------|-------------------------------|-------|--------|
|      |                               |       |        |

(b)

### Cash — No. 101

| Date | Explanation | Ref. | Debit | Credit | Balance |
|------|-------------|------|-------|--------|---------|
|      |             |      |       |        |         |
|      |             |      |       |        |         |
|      |             |      |       |        |         |
|      |             |      |       |        |         |
|      |             |      |       |        |         |
|      |             |      |       |        |         |
|      |             |      |       |        |         |
|      |             |      |       |        |         |
|      |             |      |       |        |         |
|      |             |      |       |        |         |

### Accounts Receivable — No. 112

| Date | Explanation | Ref. | Debit | Credit | Balance |
|------|-------------|------|-------|--------|---------|
|      |             |      |       |        |         |
|      |             |      |       |        |         |
|      |             |      |       |        |         |
|      |             |      |       |        |         |

### Supplies — No. 126

| Date | Explanation | Ref. | Debit | Credit | Balance |
|------|-------------|------|-------|--------|---------|
|      |             |      |       |        |         |
|      |             |      |       |        |         |

### Office Equipment — No. 151

| Date | Explanation | Ref. | Debit | Credit | Balance |
|------|-------------|------|-------|--------|---------|
|      |             |      |       |        |         |
|      |             |      |       |        |         |

### Accounts Payable — No. 201

| Date | Explanation | Ref. | Debit | Credit | Balance |
|------|-------------|------|-------|--------|---------|
|      |             |      |       |        |         |
|      |             |      |       |        |         |
|      |             |      |       |        |         |
|      |             |      |       |        |         |
|      |             |      |       |        |         |

### Unearned Revenue — No. 209

| Date | Explanation | Ref. | Debit | Credit | Balance |
|------|-------------|------|-------|--------|---------|
|      |             |      |       |        |         |
|      |             |      |       |        |         |

### F. Virmani, Capital — No. 301

| Date | Explanation | Ref. | Debit | Credit | Balance |
|------|-------------|------|-------|--------|---------|
|      |             |      |       |        |         |
|      |             |      |       |        |         |

Name:                                                                                                      Problem 2-4A Continued (2)

(b) (Continued)

**F. Virmani, Drawings**          No. 306

| Date | Explanation | Ref. | Debit | Credit | Balance |
|------|-------------|------|-------|--------|---------|
|      |             |      |       |        |         |
|      |             |      |       |        |         |

**Service Revenue**          No. 400

| Date | Explanation | Ref. | Debit | Credit | Balance |
|------|-------------|------|-------|--------|---------|
|      |             |      |       |        |         |
|      |             |      |       |        |         |
|      |             |      |       |        |         |

**Rent Expense**          No. 726

| Date | Explanation | Ref. | Debit | Credit | Balance |
|------|-------------|------|-------|--------|---------|
|      |             |      |       |        |         |
|      |             |      |       |        |         |

**Salaries Expense**          No. 729

| Date | Explanation | Ref. | Debit | Credit | Balance |
|------|-------------|------|-------|--------|---------|
|      |             |      |       |        |         |
|      |             |      |       |        |         |

**Telephone Expense**          No. 737

| Date | Explanation | Ref. | Debit | Credit | Balance |
|------|-------------|------|-------|--------|---------|
|      |             |      |       |        |         |
|      |             |      |       |        |         |

(c)

|  | Debit | Credit |
|--|-------|--------|
|  |       |        |
|  |       |        |
|  |       |        |
|  |       |        |
|  |       |        |
|  |       |        |
|  |       |        |
|  |       |        |
|  |       |        |
|  |       |        |
|  |       |        |
|  |       |        |
|  |       |        |
|  |       |        |
|  |       |        |
|  |       |        |
|  |       |        |

*Taking It Further*

## (a) General Journal

| Date | Account Titles and Explanation | Debit | Credit |
|---|---|---|---|
| | | | |

Name: _____                                    Problem 2-5A Continued (1)

(a)

## General Journal

| Date | Account Titles and Explanation | Debit | Credit |
|------|-------------------------------|-------|--------|
|      |                               |       |        |
|      |                               |       |        |
|      |                               |       |        |
|      |                               |       |        |
|      |                               |       |        |
|      |                               |       |        |
|      |                               |       |        |
|      |                               |       |        |
|      |                               |       |        |
|      |                               |       |        |
|      |                               |       |        |
|      |                               |       |        |
|      |                               |       |        |
|      |                               |       |        |
|      |                               |       |        |
|      |                               |       |        |

(b)

| Cash | Prepaid Rent |
|------|--------------|

| | Office Equipment |
|---|---|

| Accounts Receivable | Unearned Service Revenue |
|---------------------|--------------------------|

| Supplies | Accounts Payable |
|----------|------------------|

| Prepaid Insurance | Notes Payable |
|-------------------|---------------|

*Accounting Principles, 5th Canadian Edition*                     *Working Papers, Chapter 2*

Name: Problem 2-5A Continued (2)

**(b) (Continued)**

J. Abramson, Capital

Rent Expense

J. Abramson, Drawings

Salaries Expense

Service Revenue

Telephone Expense

Interest Expense

**(c)**

|  | Debit | Credit |
|---|---|---|
|  |  |  |
|  |  |  |
|  |  |  |
|  |  |  |
|  |  |  |
|  |  |  |
|  |  |  |
|  |  |  |
|  |  |  |
|  |  |  |
|  |  |  |
|  |  |  |
|  |  |  |
|  |  |  |
|  |  |  |
|  |  |  |
|  |  |  |
|  |  |  |

*Accounting Principles, 5th Canadian Edition* — *Working Papers, Chapter 2*

*Taking It Further*

**Problem 2-6A**

(a) General Journal

| Date | Account Titles and Explanation | Debit | Credit |
|------|-------------------------------|-------|--------|
|      |                               |       |        |

Name:        Problem 2-6A Continued (1)

(b) and (c)

### Cash

| Date | Explanation | Ref. | Debit | Credit | Balance |
|---|---|---|---|---|---|
| June 1 | Balance | √ | | | 15,000 |
| | | | | | |
| | | | | | |
| | | | | | |
| | | | | | |
| | | | | | |
| | | | | | |
| | | | | | |
| | | | | | |
| | | | | | |
| | | | | | |
| | | | | | |
| | | | | | |
| | | | | | |

### Accounts Receivable

| Date | Explanation | Ref. | Debit | Credit | Balance |
|---|---|---|---|---|---|
| | | | | | |
| | | | | | |
| | | | | | |

### Land

| Date | Explanation | Ref. | Debit | Credit | Balance |
|---|---|---|---|---|---|
| June 1 | Balance | √ | | | 85,000 |
| | | | | | |

### Buildings

| Date | Explanation | Ref. | Debit | Credit | Balance |
|---|---|---|---|---|---|
| June 1 | Balance | √ | | | 70,000 |
| | | | | | |

### Equipment

| Date | Explanation | Ref. | Debit | Credit | Balance |
|---|---|---|---|---|---|
| June 1 | Balance | √ | | | 20,000 |
| | | | | | |

### Accounts Payable

| Date | Explanation | Ref. | Debit | Credit | Balance |
|---|---|---|---|---|---|
| June 1 | Balance | √ | | | 5,000 |
| | | | | | |
| | | | | | |
| | | | | | |
| | | | | | |
| | | | | | |

*Accounting Principles, 5th Canadian Edition*

Name:        Problem 2-6A Continued (2)

(b) and (c) (Continued)

### Mortgage Payable

| Date | Explanation | Ref. | Debit | Credit | Balance |
|---|---|---|---|---|---|
| June 1 | Balance | √ | | | 118,000 |
| | | | | | |
| | | | | | |

### N. Fedkovych, Capital

| Date | Explanation | Ref. | Debit | Credit | Balance |
|---|---|---|---|---|---|
| June 1 | Balance | √ | | | 67,000 |
| | | | | | |

### Admission Revenue

| Date | Explanation | Ref. | Debit | Credit | Balance |
|---|---|---|---|---|---|
| | | | | | |
| | | | | | |
| | | | | | |
| | | | | | |
| | | | | | |

### Concession Revenue

| Date | Explanation | Ref. | Debit | Credit | Balance |
|---|---|---|---|---|---|
| | | | | | |
| | | | | | |
| | | | | | |
| | | | | | |

### Advertising Expense

| Date | Explanation | Ref. | Debit | Credit | Balance |
|---|---|---|---|---|---|
| | | | | | |
| | | | | | |

### Film Rental Expense

| Date | Explanation | Ref. | Debit | Credit | Balance |
|---|---|---|---|---|---|
| | | | | | |
| | | | | | |
| | | | | | |

### Interest Expense

| Date | Explanation | Ref. | Debit | Credit | Balance |
|---|---|---|---|---|---|
| | | | | | |
| | | | | | |

### Salaries Expense

| Date | Explanation | Ref. | Debit | Credit | Balance |
|---|---|---|---|---|---|
| | | | | | |
| | | | | | |

**Problem 2-6A Concluded**

(d)

|  | Debit | Credit |
|---|---|---|
|  |  |  |

*Taking It Further*

**Problem 2-7A**

(a)

## General Journal

| Date | Account Titles and Explanation | Debit | Credit |
|------|-------------------------------|-------|--------|
|      |                               |       |        |

Name:     Problem 2-7A Continued (1)

(b) and (c)

Cash

**Problem 2-7A Continued (2)**

(b) and (c) (Continued)

**Problem 2-7A Concluded**

(d)

|  | Debit | Credit |
|---|---|---|
|  |  |  |

*Taking It Further*

Problem 2-8A

(a)

(b)

Name: _____    Problem 2-8A Concluded

(c)

|  |  |  |
|---|---|---|
|  |  |  |
|  |  |  |
|  |  |  |
|  |  |  |
|  |  |  |
|  |  |  |
|  |  |  |
|  |  |  |
|  |  |  |
|  |  |  |
|  |  |  |
|  |  |  |
|  |  |  |
|  |  |  |
|  |  |  |
|  |  |  |
|  |  |  |
|  |  |  |
|  |  |  |
|  |  |  |
|  |  |  |
|  |  |  |
|  |  |  |
|  |  |  |
|  |  |  |

*Taking It Further*

**Problem 2-9A**

(a) General Journal

| Date | Account Titles and Explanation | Debit | Credit |
|------|-------------------------------|-------|--------|
|      |                               |       |        |

Name:                                            Problem 2-9A Continued (1)

(b) and (c)

Cash

Name:  Problem 2-9A Continued (2)

(b) and (c) (Continued)

(d)

|  | Debit | Credit |
|---|---|---|
|  |  |  |

*Taking It Further*

Name:                                                                                              Problem 2-10A

(a)

|  |  |  |
|---|---|---|
|  |  |  |
|  |  |  |
|  |  |  |
|  |  |  |
|  |  |  |
|  |  |  |
|  |  |  |
|  |  |  |
|  |  |  |
|  |  |  |
|  |  |  |
|  |  |  |
|  |  |  |
|  |  |  |
|  |  |  |
|  |  |  |
|  |  |  |
|  |  |  |
|  |  |  |
|  |  |  |
|  |  |  |
|  |  |  |
|  |  |  |

(b)

|  |  |  |
|---|---|---|
|  |  |  |
|  |  |  |
|  |  |  |
|  |  |  |
|  |  |  |
|  |  |  |
|  |  |  |
|  |  |  |
|  |  |  |
|  |  |  |
|  |  |  |

*Accounting Principles, 5th Canadian Edition*            *Working Papers, Chapter 2*

(c)

*Taking It Further*

Name:     Problem 2-11A

(a)

|  | Debit | Credit |
|---|---|---|
|  |  |  |
|  |  |  |
|  |  |  |
|  |  |  |
|  |  |  |
|  |  |  |
|  |  |  |
|  |  |  |
|  |  |  |
|  |  |  |
|  |  |  |
|  |  |  |
|  |  |  |
|  |  |  |
|  |  |  |
|  |  |  |
|  |  |  |
|  |  |  |
|  |  |  |
|  |  |  |
|  |  |  |
|  |  |  |
|  |  |  |
|  |  |  |
|  |  |  |
|  |  |  |
|  |  |  |
|  |  |  |
|  |  |  |
|  |  |  |

(b)

|  |  |  |
|---|---|---|
|  |  |  |
|  |  |  |
|  |  |  |
|  |  |  |
|  |  |  |
|  |  |  |
|  |  |  |
|  |  |  |
|  |  |  |
|  |  |  |
|  |  |  |
|  |  |  |
|  |  |  |
|  |  |  |

*Accounting Principles, 5th Canadian Edition*

Name:                                                                                    Problem 2-11A Concluded

**(b) (Continued)**

|  |  |  |
|---|---|---|
|  |  |  |
|  |  |  |
|  |  |  |
|  |  |  |
|  |  |  |

|  |  |  |
|---|---|---|
|  |  |  |
|  |  |  |
|  |  |  |
|  |  |  |
|  |  |  |
|  |  |  |
|  |  |  |
|  |  |  |
|  |  |  |
|  |  |  |
|  |  |  |
|  |  |  |
|  |  |  |
|  |  |  |
|  |  |  |
|  |  |  |
|  |  |  |
|  |  |  |
|  |  |  |
|  |  |  |
|  |  |  |
|  |  |  |

*Taking It Further*

Name: _____                                                     Problem 2-12A

**(a)**

| | | | | | |
|---|---|---|---|---|---|

**(b)**

| Trans. | 1. Balance? | 2. Accounts in Error? | 3. O or U? | 4. Debit Column? | 5. Credit Column? |
|---|---|---|---|---|---|
| 1. | | | | | |
| 2. | | | | | |
| 3. | | | | | |
| 4. | | | | | |
| 5. | | | | | |
| 6. | | | | | |
| 7. | | | | | |
| 8. | | | | | |
| 9. | | | | | |
| 10. | | | | | |

*Accounting Principles, 5th Canadian Edition*                                           *Working Papers, Chapter 2*

*Taking It Further*

# Problem 2-13A

|  | Debit | Credit |
|---|---|---|
|  |  |  |
|  |  |  |
|  |  |  |
|  |  |  |
|  |  |  |
|  |  |  |
|  |  |  |
|  |  |  |
|  |  |  |
|  |  |  |
|  |  |  |
|  |  |  |
|  |  |  |
|  |  |  |
|  |  |  |
|  |  |  |
|  |  |  |
|  |  |  |
|  |  |  |
|  |  |  |
|  |  |  |
|  |  |  |
|  |  |  |
|  |  |  |

*Taking It Further*

(a) General Journal

| Date | Account Titles and Explanation | Debit | Credit |
|------|-------------------------------|-------|--------|
|      |                               |       |        |

**Continuing Cookie Chronicle Continued (1)**

(b) Cash

| Date | Explanation | Ref. | Debit | Credit | Balance |
|------|-------------|------|-------|--------|---------|
|      |             |      |       |        |         |
|      |             |      |       |        |         |
|      |             |      |       |        |         |
|      |             |      |       |        |         |
|      |             |      |       |        |         |
|      |             |      |       |        |         |
|      |             |      |       |        |         |
|      |             |      |       |        |         |
|      |             |      |       |        |         |
|      |             |      |       |        |         |
|      |             |      |       |        |         |
|      |             |      |       |        |         |
|      |             |      |       |        |         |

| Date | Explanation | Ref. | Debit | Credit | Balance |
|------|-------------|------|-------|--------|---------|
|      |             |      |       |        |         |
|      |             |      |       |        |         |
|      |             |      |       |        |         |
|      |             |      |       |        |         |

| Date | Explanation | Ref. | Debit | Credit | Balance |
|------|-------------|------|-------|--------|---------|
|      |             |      |       |        |         |
|      |             |      |       |        |         |
|      |             |      |       |        |         |

| Date | Explanation | Ref. | Debit | Credit | Balance |
|------|-------------|------|-------|--------|---------|
|      |             |      |       |        |         |
|      |             |      |       |        |         |
|      |             |      |       |        |         |

| Date | Explanation | Ref. | Debit | Credit | Balance |
|------|-------------|------|-------|--------|---------|
|      |             |      |       |        |         |
|      |             |      |       |        |         |
|      |             |      |       |        |         |

| Date | Explanation | Ref. | Debit | Credit | Balance |
|------|-------------|------|-------|--------|---------|
|      |             |      |       |        |         |
|      |             |      |       |        |         |
|      |             |      |       |        |         |

*Accounting Principles, 5th Canadian Edition*

Name:                                                        Continuing Cookie Chronicle Continued (2)

(b) (Continued)

| Date | Explanation | Ref. | Debit | Credit | Balance |
|------|-------------|------|-------|--------|---------|
|      |             |      |       |        |         |
|      |             |      |       |        |         |
|      |             |      |       |        |         |

| Date | Explanation | Ref. | Debit | Credit | Balance |
|------|-------------|------|-------|--------|---------|
|      |             |      |       |        |         |
|      |             |      |       |        |         |
|      |             |      |       |        |         |
|      |             |      |       |        |         |

| Date | Explanation | Ref. | Debit | Credit | Balance |
|------|-------------|------|-------|--------|---------|
|      |             |      |       |        |         |
|      |             |      |       |        |         |
|      |             |      |       |        |         |
|      |             |      |       |        |         |

| Date | Explanation | Ref. | Debit | Credit | Balance |
|------|-------------|------|-------|--------|---------|
|      |             |      |       |        |         |
|      |             |      |       |        |         |
|      |             |      |       |        |         |

| Date | Explanation | Ref. | Debit | Credit | Balance |
|------|-------------|------|-------|--------|---------|
|      |             |      |       |        |         |
|      |             |      |       |        |         |
|      |             |      |       |        |         |

| Date | Explanation | Ref. | Debit | Credit | Balance |
|------|-------------|------|-------|--------|---------|
|      |             |      |       |        |         |
|      |             |      |       |        |         |
|      |             |      |       |        |         |

| Date | Explanation | Ref. | Debit | Credit | Balance |
|------|-------------|------|-------|--------|---------|
|      |             |      |       |        |         |
|      |             |      |       |        |         |
|      |             |      |       |        |         |

*Accounting Principles, 5th Canadian Edition*                                              *Working Papers, Chapter 2*

**Name:** Continuing Cookie Chronicle Concluded

(c)

| | Debit | Credit |
|---|---|---|
| | | |

# Brief Exercises 3-1 to 3-3

## BE3-1

|  | Cash | Profit |
|---|---|---|
| (a) | -$100 | $0 |
| (b) | | |
| (c) | | |
| (d) | | |
| (e) | | |
| (f) | | |
| (g) | | |
| (h) | | |
| (i) | | |

## BE3-2

(a)  (b)

1.
2.
3.
4.
5.
6.
7.
8.

## BE3-3

A Co.   Supplies used




B Co.   Supplies on hand

**BE3-4**

|  |
|---|

Cleaning Supplies | Cleaning Supplies Expense

**BE3-5**

Name                                                                                   Brief Exercise 3-6

**(a) and (b)**

**(c)**

| | CREED CO. | |
|---|---|---|
| | Balance Sheet (partial) | |
| | December 31 | |
| | 2011 | 2010 |
| | | |
| | | |
| | | |
| | | |
| | | |
| | | |
| | | |
| | | |
| | | |
| | | |

| | CREED CO. | |
|---|---|---|
| | Income Statement (partial) | |
| | Year Ended December 31 | |
| | 2011 | 2010 |
| | | |
| | | |
| | | |
| | | |
| | | |
| | | |

*Accounting Principles, 5th Canadian Edition*

## BE3-8

**General Journal**

| Date | Account Titles and Explanation | Debit | Credit |
|------|-------------------------------|-------|--------|
|      |                               |       |        |

## BE3-9

**General Journal**

| Date | Account Titles and Explanation | Debit | Credit |
|------|-------------------------------|-------|--------|
|      |                               |       |        |

**BE3-10**

### General Journal

| | Account Titles and Explanation | Debit | Credit |
|---|---|---|---|
| | | | |

**BE3-11**

### General Journal

| Date | Account Titles and Explanation | Debit | Credit |
|---|---|---|---|
| | | | |

Name  Brief Exercises 3-12 to 3-13

| BE3-12 | Assets | Liabilities | Owner's Equity | Revenue | Expenses | Profit |
|---|---|---|---|---|---|---|
| Prepaid expenses | | | | | | |
| Unearned revenues | | | | | | |
| Accrued revenues | | | | | | |
| Accrued expenses | | | | | | |

| BE3-13 | (a) WINTERHOLT COMPANY<br>Adjusted Trial Balance<br>September 30, 2011 | | (b) A, L, C, D, R, or E | (c) IS, OE, or BS |
|---|---|---|---|---|
| | Debit | Credit | | |
| | | | | |
| | | | | |
| | | | | |
| | | | | |
| | | | | |
| | | | | |
| | | | | |
| | | | | |
| | | | | |
| | | | | |
| | | | | |
| | | | | |
| | | | | |
| | | | | |
| | | | | |
| | | | | |
| | | | | |
| | | | | |
| | | | | |
| | | | | |
| | | | | |
| | | | | |
| | | | | |
| | | | | |
| | | | | |
| | | | | |
| | | | | |

*Accounting Principles, 5th Canadian Edition*

Name                                                              *Brief Exercises 3-14 to 3-15

**\*BE3-14 (a)**          General Journal

| Date | Account Titles and Explanation | Debit | Credit |
|---|---|---|---|
| | | | |
| | | | |
| | | | |
| | | | |
| | | | |
| | | | |

                 Cleaning Supplies                            Cleaning Supplies Expense

**(b)**

---

**\*BE3-15 (a)**          General Journal

| Date | Account Titles and Explanation | Debit | Credit |
|---|---|---|---|
| | | | |
| | | | |
| | | | |
| | | | |
| | | | |

             Unearned Insurance Revenue                     Insurance Revenue

**(b)**

*Accounting Principles, 5th Canadian Edition*

**E3-1**

**E3-2**
(a)
(b)
(c)
(d)
(e)
(f)
(g)

Name  Exercise 3-3

## Income Statement

| Item | Type of Account | Account Name | Increase or Decrease | Impact on Profit |
|---|---|---|---|---|
|  |  |  |  |  |
| 1. | Expense | Interest Expense | Increase | Decrease |
| 2. |  |  |  |  |
| 3. |  |  |  |  |
| 4. |  |  |  |  |
| 5. |  |  |  |  |
| 6. |  |  |  |  |
| 7. |  |  |  |  |
| 8. |  |  |  |  |
|  |  |  |  |  |

## Balance Sheet

| Item | Type of Account | Account Name | Increase or Decrease | Impact on Owner's Equity |
|---|---|---|---|---|
|  |  |  |  |  |
| 1. | Liability | Interest Payable | Increase | Decrease |
| 2. |  |  |  |  |
| 3. |  |  |  |  |
| 4. |  |  |  |  |
| 5. |  |  |  |  |
| 6. |  |  |  |  |
| 7. |  |  |  |  |
| 8. |  |  |  |  |
|  |  |  |  |  |

*Accounting Principles, 5th Canadian Edition*  *Working Papers, Chapter 3*

Exercise 3-4

**(a) and (b)** General Journal

| Date | Account Titles and Explanation | Debit | Credit |
|------|-------------------------------|-------|--------|
|      |                               |       |        |

(c)

Name            Exercise 3-5

(a)

**General Journal**

| Date | Account Titles and Explanation | Debit | Credit |
|------|-------------------------------|-------|--------|
|      |                               |       |        |

(b)

|  | Furniture | Lighting Equipment | Computer Equipment |
|--|-----------|--------------------|--------------------|
|  |           |                    |                    |

*Accounting Principles, 5th Canadian Edition*      *Working Papers, Chapter 3*

Name                                                                                                    Exercise 3-6

| Date | Account Titles and Explanation | Debit | Credit |
|------|-------------------------------|-------|--------|
|      |                               |       |        |

# Exercise 3-7

## General Journal

| Date | Account Titles and Explanation | Debit | Credit |
|------|-------------------------------|-------|--------|
|      |                               |       |        |

# General Journal

| Date | Account Titles and Explanation | Debit | Credit |
|------|-------------------------------|-------|--------|
|      |                               |       |        |

# General Journal

| Date | Account Titles and Explanation | Debit | Credit |
|------|-------------------------------|-------|--------|
|      |                               |       |        |

Exercise 3-11

Name *Exercise 3-12

(a) and (b)

## General Journal

| Date | Account Titles and Explanation | Debit | Credit |
|------|-------------------------------|-------|--------|
|      |                               |       |        |

*Exercise 3-12 Concluded

(c)

(d)

Name                                                          *Exercise 3-13

(a) **General Journal**

| Date | Account Titles and Explanation | Debit | Credit |
|------|-------------------------------|-------|--------|
|      |                               |       |        |

Name *Exercise 3-13 Concluded

(b) General Journal

| Date | Account Titles and Explanation | Debit | Credit |
|------|-------------------------------|-------|--------|
|      |                               |       |        |

(c)

(a) and (b)

**Problem 3-1A Concluded**

**(a) and (b) Concluded**

**Taking It Further**

**Problem 3-2A**

**1. (a)**

### General Journal

| Date | Account Titles and Explanation | Debit | Credit |
|------|-------------------------------|-------|--------|
|      |                               |       |        |
|      |                               |       |        |
|      |                               |       |        |
|      |                               |       |        |
|      |                               |       |        |
|      |                               |       |        |
|      |                               |       |        |
|      |                               |       |        |
|      |                               |       |        |
|      |                               |       |        |
|      |                               |       |        |
|      |                               |       |        |
|      |                               |       |        |
|      |                               |       |        |

**1. (b)**

Office Supplies | Supplies Expense

**2. (a)**

| | | | |
|---|---|---|---|
| | | | |

**2. (b)**

Equipment | Accumulated Depreciation-Equipment

**Problem 3-2A Continued (1)**

**3. (a)** General Journal

| Date | Account Titles and Explanation | Debit | Credit |
|------|-------------------------------|-------|--------|
|      |                               |       |        |
|      |                               |       |        |
|      |                               |       |        |
|      |                               |       |        |
|      |                               |       |        |
|      |                               |       |        |
|      |                               |       |        |
|      |                               |       |        |
|      |                               |       |        |
|      |                               |       |        |
|      |                               |       |        |
|      |                               |       |        |
|      |                               |       |        |

**3. (b)**

Prepaid Insurance | Insurance Expense

**4. (a)**

|  |  |  |
|--|--|--|
|  |  |  |

**4. (b)**

Prepaid Truck rental | Truck Rent Expense

*Accounting Principles, 5th Canadian Edition*

Name                                                              Problem 3-2A Concluded

**5. (a)** General Journal

| Date | Account Titles and Explanation | Debit | Credit |
|------|-------------------------------|-------|--------|
|      |                               |       |        |
|      |                               |       |        |
|      |                               |       |        |
|      |                               |       |        |
|      |                               |       |        |
|      |                               |       |        |
|      |                               |       |        |
|      |                               |       |        |
|      |                               |       |        |
|      |                               |       |        |
|      |                               |       |        |

**5. (b)**

| Unearned Service Revenue | Service Revenue |
|--------------------------|-----------------|
|                          |                 |

**6. (a)**

|   |   |   |
|---|---|---|
|   |   |   |
|   |   |   |
|   |   |   |
|   |   |   |
|   |   |   |
|   |   |   |
|   |   |   |
|   |   |   |
|   |   |   |
|   |   |   |

**6. (b)**

| Unearned Rent Revenue | Rent Revenue |
|-----------------------|--------------|
|                       |              |

**Taking It Further**

Name	Problem 3-3A

| | General Journal | | |
|---|---|---|---|
| Date | Account Titles and Explanation | Debit | Credit |
| | | | |

**Problem 3-3A Concluded**

## General Journal

| Date | Account Titles and Explanation | Debit | Credit |
|------|-------------------------------|-------|--------|
|      |                               |       |        |
|      |                               |       |        |
|      |                               |       |        |
|      |                               |       |        |
|      |                               |       |        |
|      |                               |       |        |
|      |                               |       |        |
|      |                               |       |        |
|      |                               |       |        |
|      |                               |       |        |
|      |                               |       |        |
|      |                               |       |        |
|      |                               |       |        |
|      |                               |       |        |

*Taking It Further*

## General Journal

| Date | Account Titles and Explanation | Debit | Credit |
|------|-------------------------------|-------|--------|
|      |                               |       |        |

**Problem 3-4A Concluded**

| General Journal | | | |
|---|---|---|---|
| Date | Account Titles and Explanation | Debit | Credit |
| | | | |
| | | | |
| | | | |
| | | | |
| | | | |
| | | | |
| | | | |
| | | | |
| | | | |
| | | | |
| | | | |
| | | | |
| | | | |
| | | | |
| | | | |
| | | | |
| | | | |
| | | | |
| | | | |
| | | | |
| | | | |
| | | | |

*Taking It Further*

Name                                                                 Problem 3-5A

| | General Journal | | |
|---|---|---|---|
| Date | Account Titles and Explanation | Debit | Credit |
| | | | |

*Taking It Further*

Problem 3-6A

**(a)** General Journal

| Date | Account Titles and Explanation | Debit | Credit |
|---|---|---|---|
| | | | |

**(b)**

*Taking It Further*

Problem 3-7A

(a)

(b)

**Problem 3-7A Concluded**

(b) (Continued)

*Taking It Further*

# General Journal

| Date | Account Titles and Explanation | Debit | Credit |
|---|---|---|---|
| | | | |

Name                                                                 Problem 3-8A Continued (1)

(b)

### Cash

| Date | Explanation | Ref. | Debit | Credit | Balance |
|------|-------------|------|-------|--------|---------|
|      |             |      |       |        |         |
|      |             |      |       |        |         |
|      |             |      |       |        |         |
|      |             |      |       |        |         |
|      |             |      |       |        |         |

### Accounts Receivable

| Date | Explanation | Ref. | Debit | Credit | Balance |
|------|-------------|------|-------|--------|---------|
|      |             |      |       |        |         |
|      |             |      |       |        |         |
|      |             |      |       |        |         |

### Prepaid Insurance

| Date | Explanation | Ref. | Debit | Credit | Balance |
|------|-------------|------|-------|--------|---------|
|      |             |      |       |        |         |
|      |             |      |       |        |         |
|      |             |      |       |        |         |

### Supplies

| Date | Explanation | Ref. | Debit | Credit | Balance |
|------|-------------|------|-------|--------|---------|
|      |             |      |       |        |         |
|      |             |      |       |        |         |
|      |             |      |       |        |         |

### Office Equipment

| Date | Explanation | Ref. | Debit | Credit | Balance |
|------|-------------|------|-------|--------|---------|
|      |             |      |       |        |         |
|      |             |      |       |        |         |
|      |             |      |       |        |         |

### Accumulated Depreciation-Office Equipment

| Date | Explanation | Ref. | Debit | Credit | Balance |
|------|-------------|------|-------|--------|---------|
|      |             |      |       |        |         |
|      |             |      |       |        |         |
|      |             |      |       |        |         |

### Buses

| Date | Explanation | Ref. | Debit | Credit | Balance |
|------|-------------|------|-------|--------|---------|
|      |             |      |       |        |         |
|      |             |      |       |        |         |
|      |             |      |       |        |         |

### Accumulated Depreciation-Buses

| Date | Explanation | Ref. | Debit | Credit | Balance |
|------|-------------|------|-------|--------|---------|
|      |             |      |       |        |         |
|      |             |      |       |        |         |
|      |             |      |       |        |         |

*Accounting Principles, 5th Canadian Edition*

Name                                                                                                       Problem 3-8A Continued (2)

(b)

### Accounts Payable

| Date | Explanation | Ref. | Debit | Credit | Balance |
|------|-------------|------|-------|--------|---------|
|      |             |      |       |        |         |
|      |             |      |       |        |         |
|      |             |      |       |        |         |
|      |             |      |       |        |         |

### Notes Payable

| Date | Explanation | Ref. | Debit | Credit | Balance |
|------|-------------|------|-------|--------|---------|
|      |             |      |       |        |         |
|      |             |      |       |        |         |
|      |             |      |       |        |         |

### Interest Payable

| Date | Explanation | Ref. | Debit | Credit | Balance |
|------|-------------|------|-------|--------|---------|
|      |             |      |       |        |         |
|      |             |      |       |        |         |
|      |             |      |       |        |         |

### Salaries Payable

| Date | Explanation | Ref. | Debit | Credit | Balance |
|------|-------------|------|-------|--------|---------|
|      |             |      |       |        |         |
|      |             |      |       |        |         |
|      |             |      |       |        |         |

### Unearned Fees

| Date | Explanation | Ref. | Debit | Credit | Balance |
|------|-------------|------|-------|--------|---------|
|      |             |      |       |        |         |
|      |             |      |       |        |         |
|      |             |      |       |        |         |

### F. Rosenthal, Capital

| Date | Explanation | Ref. | Debit | Credit | Balance |
|------|-------------|------|-------|--------|---------|
|      |             |      |       |        |         |
|      |             |      |       |        |         |
|      |             |      |       |        |         |

### F. Rosenthal, Drawings

| Date | Explanation | Ref. | Debit | Credit | Balance |
|------|-------------|------|-------|--------|---------|
|      |             |      |       |        |         |
|      |             |      |       |        |         |
|      |             |      |       |        |         |

### Fees Earned

| Date | Explanation | Ref. | Debit | Credit | Balance |
|------|-------------|------|-------|--------|---------|
|      |             |      |       |        |         |
|      |             |      |       |        |         |
|      |             |      |       |        |         |
|      |             |      |       |        |         |

**Problem 3-8A Continued (3)**

(b)

### Advertising Expense

| Date | Explanation | Ref. | Debit | Credit | Balance |
|------|-------------|------|-------|--------|---------|
|      |             |      |       |        |         |
|      |             |      |       |        |         |
|      |             |      |       |        |         |

### Depreciation Expense

| Date | Explanation | Ref. | Debit | Credit | Balance |
|------|-------------|------|-------|--------|---------|
|      |             |      |       |        |         |
|      |             |      |       |        |         |

### Gas and Oil Expense

| Date | Explanation | Ref. | Debit | Credit | Balance |
|------|-------------|------|-------|--------|---------|
|      |             |      |       |        |         |
|      |             |      |       |        |         |
|      |             |      |       |        |         |

### Insurance Expense

| Date | Explanation | Ref. | Debit | Credit | Balance |
|------|-------------|------|-------|--------|---------|
|      |             |      |       |        |         |
|      |             |      |       |        |         |
|      |             |      |       |        |         |

### Interest Expense

| Date | Explanation | Ref. | Debit | Credit | Balance |
|------|-------------|------|-------|--------|---------|
|      |             |      |       |        |         |
|      |             |      |       |        |         |
|      |             |      |       |        |         |

### Rent Expense

| Date | Explanation | Ref. | Debit | Credit | Balance |
|------|-------------|------|-------|--------|---------|
|      |             |      |       |        |         |
|      |             |      |       |        |         |
|      |             |      |       |        |         |

### Salaries Expense

| Date | Explanation | Ref. | Debit | Credit | Balance |
|------|-------------|------|-------|--------|---------|
|      |             |      |       |        |         |
|      |             |      |       |        |         |
|      |             |      |       |        |         |

### Supplies Expense

| Date | Explanation | Ref. | Debit | Credit | Balance |
|------|-------------|------|-------|--------|---------|
|      |             |      |       |        |         |
|      |             |      |       |        |         |
|      |             |      |       |        |         |

(c)

|  | Debit | Credit |
|---|---|---|
|  |  |  |

Taking It Further

Name  Problem 3-9A

**(a)** General Journal

| Date | Account Titles and Explanation | Debit | Credit |
|------|-------------------------------|-------|--------|
|      |                               |       |        |

Name Problem 3-9A Continued (1)

(b)

### Cash

| Date | Explanation | Ref. | Debit | Credit | Balance |
|------|-------------|------|-------|--------|---------|
|      |             |      |       |        |         |
|      |             |      |       |        |         |
|      |             |      |       |        |         |
|      |             |      |       |        |         |
|      |             |      |       |        |         |

### Accounts Receivable

| Date | Explanation | Ref. | Debit | Credit | Balance |
|------|-------------|------|-------|--------|---------|
|      |             |      |       |        |         |
|      |             |      |       |        |         |
|      |             |      |       |        |         |

### Prepaid Insurance

| Date | Explanation | Ref. | Debit | Credit | Balance |
|------|-------------|------|-------|--------|---------|
|      |             |      |       |        |         |
|      |             |      |       |        |         |
|      |             |      |       |        |         |

### Supplies

| Date | Explanation | Ref. | Debit | Credit | Balance |
|------|-------------|------|-------|--------|---------|
|      |             |      |       |        |         |
|      |             |      |       |        |         |
|      |             |      |       |        |         |

### Land

| Date | Explanation | Ref. | Debit | Credit | Balance |
|------|-------------|------|-------|--------|---------|
|      |             |      |       |        |         |
|      |             |      |       |        |         |
|      |             |      |       |        |         |

### Cottages

| Date | Explanation | Ref. | Debit | Credit | Balance |
|------|-------------|------|-------|--------|---------|
|      |             |      |       |        |         |
|      |             |      |       |        |         |
|      |             |      |       |        |         |

### Accumulated Depreciation-Cottages

| Date | Explanation | Ref. | Debit | Credit | Balance |
|------|-------------|------|-------|--------|---------|
|      |             |      |       |        |         |
|      |             |      |       |        |         |
|      |             |      |       |        |         |

### Furniture

| Date | Explanation | Ref. | Debit | Credit | Balance |
|------|-------------|------|-------|--------|---------|
|      |             |      |       |        |         |
|      |             |      |       |        |         |
|      |             |      |       |        |         |

Name  Problem 3-9A Continued (2)

(b) 

### Accumulated Depreciation-Furniture

| Date | Explanation | Ref. | Debit | Credit | Balance |
|------|-------------|------|-------|--------|---------|
|      |             |      |       |        |         |
|      |             |      |       |        |         |
|      |             |      |       |        |         |

### Accounts Payable

| Date | Explanation | Ref. | Debit | Credit | Balance |
|------|-------------|------|-------|--------|---------|
|      |             |      |       |        |         |
|      |             |      |       |        |         |
|      |             |      |       |        |         |
|      |             |      |       |        |         |

### Unearned Rent Revenue

| Date | Explanation | Ref. | Debit | Credit | Balance |
|------|-------------|------|-------|--------|---------|
|      |             |      |       |        |         |
|      |             |      |       |        |         |
|      |             |      |       |        |         |

### Salaries Payable

| Date | Explanation | Ref. | Debit | Credit | Balance |
|------|-------------|------|-------|--------|---------|
|      |             |      |       |        |         |
|      |             |      |       |        |         |
|      |             |      |       |        |         |

### Interest Payable

| Date | Explanation | Ref. | Debit | Credit | Balance |
|------|-------------|------|-------|--------|---------|
|      |             |      |       |        |         |
|      |             |      |       |        |         |
|      |             |      |       |        |         |

### Mortgage Payable

| Date | Explanation | Ref. | Debit | Credit | Balance |
|------|-------------|------|-------|--------|---------|
|      |             |      |       |        |         |
|      |             |      |       |        |         |
|      |             |      |       |        |         |

### K. MacPhail, Capital

| Date | Explanation | Ref. | Debit | Credit | Balance |
|------|-------------|------|-------|--------|---------|
|      |             |      |       |        |         |
|      |             |      |       |        |         |
|      |             |      |       |        |         |
|      |             |      |       |        |         |

### K. MacPhail, Drawings

| Date | Explanation | Ref. | Debit | Credit | Balance |
|------|-------------|------|-------|--------|---------|
|      |             |      |       |        |         |
|      |             |      |       |        |         |
|      |             |      |       |        |         |

(b)

### Rent Revenue

| Date | Explanation | Ref. | Debit | Credit | Balance |
|------|-------------|------|-------|--------|---------|
|      |             |      |       |        |         |
|      |             |      |       |        |         |
|      |             |      |       |        |         |

### Depreciation Expense

| Date | Explanation | Ref. | Debit | Credit | Balance |
|------|-------------|------|-------|--------|---------|
|      |             |      |       |        |         |
|      |             |      |       |        |         |

### Insurance Expense

| Date | Explanation | Ref. | Debit | Credit | Balance |
|------|-------------|------|-------|--------|---------|
|      |             |      |       |        |         |
|      |             |      |       |        |         |
|      |             |      |       |        |         |

### Interest Expense

| Date | Explanation | Ref. | Debit | Credit | Balance |
|------|-------------|------|-------|--------|---------|
|      |             |      |       |        |         |
|      |             |      |       |        |         |
|      |             |      |       |        |         |

### Repair Expense

| Date | Explanation | Ref. | Debit | Credit | Balance |
|------|-------------|------|-------|--------|---------|
|      |             |      |       |        |         |
|      |             |      |       |        |         |
|      |             |      |       |        |         |

### Salaries Expense

| Date | Explanation | Ref. | Debit | Credit | Balance |
|------|-------------|------|-------|--------|---------|
|      |             |      |       |        |         |
|      |             |      |       |        |         |
|      |             |      |       |        |         |

### Supplies Expense

| Date | Explanation | Ref. | Debit | Credit | Balance |
|------|-------------|------|-------|--------|---------|
|      |             |      |       |        |         |
|      |             |      |       |        |         |
|      |             |      |       |        |         |
|      |             |      |       |        |         |

### Utilities Expense

| Date | Explanation | Ref. | Debit | Credit | Balance |
|------|-------------|------|-------|--------|---------|
|      |             |      |       |        |         |
|      |             |      |       |        |         |

(c)

|  | Debit | Credit |
|---|---|---|
|  |  |  |

(d)

**(d) (Continued)**

**Taking It Further**

**Problem 3-10A**

(a) General Journal

| Date | Account Titles and Explanation | Debit | Credit |
|------|-------------------------------|-------|--------|
|      |                               |       |        |

(b)

(b) (Continued)

**(c)**

**(d)**

Salaries Payable

*Taking It Further*

Problem 3-11A

**(a) General Journal**

| Date | Account Titles and Explanation | Debit | Credit |
|------|-------------------------------|-------|--------|
|      |                               |       |        |

(b)

|  | Debit | Credit |
|---|---|---|

(c)

**Problem 3-11A Concluded**

(c) (Continued)

| | | |
|---|---|---|
| | | |

**Taking It Further**

**Problem 3-12A**

(a)

**General Journal**

| Date | Account Titles and Explanation | Debit | Credit |
|------|-------------------------------|-------|--------|
|      |                               |       |        |

| Supplies | Supplies Expense |
|----------|------------------|
|          |                  |

| Prepaid Insurance | Insurance Expense |
|-------------------|-------------------|
|                   |                   |

| Unearned Service Revenue | Service Revenue |
|--------------------------|-----------------|
|                          |                 |

Name *Problem 3-12A Concluded

**(b) General Journal**

| Date | Account Titles and Explanation | Debit | Credit |
|------|-------------------------------|-------|--------|
|      |                               |       |        |

*Taking It Further*

Accounting Principles, 5th Canadian Edition — Working Papers, Chapter 3

**Problem 3-13A**

**(a) General Journal**

| Date | Account Titles and Explanation | Debit | Credit |
|------|-------------------------------|-------|--------|
|      |                               |       |        |

(b)

|  | Debit | Credit |
|---|---|---|

(c)

| | | |
|---|---|---|
| | | |

**(c) (Continued)**

**Taking It Further**

(a)

## General Journal

| Date | Account Titles and Explanation | Debit | Credit |
|------|-------------------------------|-------|--------|
|      |                               |       |        |

## Cash

| Date | Explanation | Ref. | Debit | Credit | Balance |
|------|-------------|------|-------|--------|---------|
| Nov. 30 | Balance | √ |  |  | 1,440 |

## Accounts Receivable

| Date | Explanation | Ref. | Debit | Credit | Balance |
|------|-------------|------|-------|--------|---------|
| Nov. 30 | Balance | √ |  |  | 250 |

## Advertising Supplies

| Date | Explanation | Ref. | Debit | Credit | Balance |
|------|-------------|------|-------|--------|---------|
| Nov. 30 | Balance | √ |  |  | 175 |

## Baking Supplies

| Date | Explanation | Ref. | Debit | Credit | Balance |
|------|-------------|------|-------|--------|---------|
| Nov. 30 | Balance | √ |  |  | 135 |

(a) (Continued)

### Baking Equipment

| Date | Explanation | Ref. | Debit | Credit | Balance |
|---|---|---|---|---|---|
| Nov. 30 | Balance | √ | | | 1,400 |
| | | | | | |
| | | | | | |
| | | | | | |

### Accumulated Amortization - Baking Equipment

| Date | Explanation | Ref. | Debit | Credit | Balance |
|---|---|---|---|---|---|
| | | | | | |
| | | | | | |
| | | | | | |

### Accounts Payable

| Date | Explanation | Ref. | Debit | Credit | Balance |
|---|---|---|---|---|---|
| Nov. 30 | Balance | √ | | | 75 |
| | | | | | |
| | | | | | |
| | | | | | |

### Interest Payable

| Date | Explanation | Ref. | Debit | Credit | Balance |
|---|---|---|---|---|---|
| | | | | | |
| | | | | | |
| | | | | | |

### Unearned Revenue

| Date | Explanation | Ref. | Debit | Credit | Balance |
|---|---|---|---|---|---|
| Nov. 30 | Balance | √ | | | 25 |
| | | | | | |
| | | | | | |
| | | | | | |

### Notes Payable

| Date | Explanation | Ref. | Debit | Credit | Balance |
|---|---|---|---|---|---|
| Nov. 30 | Balance | √ | | | 2,000 |
| | | | | | |
| | | | | | |

### N. Koebel, Capital

| Date | Explanation | Ref. | Debit | Credit | Balance |
|---|---|---|---|---|---|
| Nov. 30 | Balance | √ | | | 1,000 |
| | | | | | |
| | | | | | |

Name  
(a) (Continued)

Continuing Cookie Chronicle Continued (2)

### Teaching Revenue

| Date | Explanation | Ref. | Debit | Credit | Balance |
|---|---|---|---|---|---|
| Nov. 30 | Balance | √ | | | 375 |
| | | | | | |
| | | | | | |
| | | | | | |
| | | | | | |

### Telephone Expense

| Date | Explanation | Ref. | Debit | Credit | Balance |
|---|---|---|---|---|---|
| | | | | | |
| | | | | | |
| | | | | | |

### Advertising Supplies Expense

| Date | Explanation | Ref. | Debit | Credit | Balance |
|---|---|---|---|---|---|
| | | | | | |
| | | | | | |
| | | | | | |

### Baking Supplies Expense

| Date | Explanation | Ref. | Debit | Credit | Balance |
|---|---|---|---|---|---|
| | | | | | |
| | | | | | |
| | | | | | |

### Depreciation Expense

| Date | Explanation | Ref. | Debit | Credit | Balance |
|---|---|---|---|---|---|
| | | | | | |
| | | | | | |
| | | | | | |

### Interest Expense

| Date | Explanation | Ref. | Debit | Credit | Balance |
|---|---|---|---|---|---|
| | | | | | |
| | | | | | |
| | | | | | |

| Date | Explanation | Ref. | Debit | Credit | Balance |
|---|---|---|---|---|---|
| | | | | | |
| | | | | | |
| | | | | | |

*Accounting Principles, 5th Canadian Edition*

**(b)**

|  | Debit | Credit |
|---|---|---|
|  |  |  |
|  |  |  |
|  |  |  |
|  |  |  |
|  |  |  |
|  |  |  |
|  |  |  |
|  |  |  |
|  |  |  |
|  |  |  |
|  |  |  |
|  |  |  |
|  |  |  |
|  |  |  |
|  |  |  |
|  |  |  |
|  |  |  |
|  |  |  |
|  |  |  |
|  |  |  |
|  |  |  |
|  |  |  |
|  |  |  |
|  |  |  |
|  |  |  |

**(c)**

|  |  |  |
|---|---|---|
|  |  |  |
|  |  |  |
|  |  |  |
|  |  |  |
|  |  |  |
|  |  |  |
|  |  |  |
|  |  |  |
|  |  |  |
|  |  |  |
|  |  |  |
|  |  |  |
|  |  |  |
|  |  |  |
|  |  |  |

(d)

Name  Cumulative Coverage

(a), (c), and (e)

### Cash

| Date | Explanation | Ref. | Debit | Credit | Balance |
|---|---|---|---|---|---|
| Sept. 1 | Balance | √ | | | 1,880 |
| | | | | | |
| | | | | | |
| | | | | | |
| | | | | | |
| | | | | | |
| | | | | | |
| | | | | | |
| | | | | | |
| | | | | | |
| | | | | | |
| | | | | | |

### Accounts Receivable

| Date | Explanation | Ref. | Debit | Credit | Balance |
|---|---|---|---|---|---|
| Sept. 1 | Balance | √ | | | 3,720 |
| | | | | | |
| | | | | | |
| | | | | | |
| | | | | | |

### Supplies

| Date | Explanation | Ref. | Debit | Credit | Balance |
|---|---|---|---|---|---|
| Sept. 1 | Balance | √ | | | 800 |
| | | | | | |
| | | | | | |
| | | | | | |
| | | | | | |

### Store Equipment

| Date | Explanation | Ref. | Debit | Credit | Balance |
|---|---|---|---|---|---|
| Sept. 1 | Balance | √ | | | 15,000 |
| | | | | | |
| | | | | | |
| | | | | | |

### Accumulated Depreciation - Store Equipment

| Date | Explanation | Ref. | Debit | Credit | Balance |
|---|---|---|---|---|---|
| Sept. 1 | Balance | √ | | | 1,500 |
| | | | | | |
| | | | | | |
| | | | | | |

**(a), (c), and (e) (Continued)**

### Accounts Payable

| Date | Explanation | Ref. | Debit | Credit | Balance |
|---|---|---|---|---|---|
| Sept. 1 | Balance | √ | | | 3,100 |
| | | | | | |
| | | | | | |
| | | | | | |
| | | | | | |

### Unearned Service Revenue

| Date | Explanation | Ref. | Debit | Credit | Balance |
|---|---|---|---|---|---|
| Sept. 1 | Balance | √ | | | 400 |
| | | | | | |
| | | | | | |
| | | | | | |
| | | | | | |

### Salaries Payable

| Date | Explanation | Ref. | Debit | Credit | Balance |
|---|---|---|---|---|---|
| Sept. 1 | Balance | √ | | | 700 |
| | | | | | |
| | | | | | |
| | | | | | |

### Interest Payable

| Date | Explanation | Ref. | Debit | Credit | Balance |
|---|---|---|---|---|---|
| | | | | | |
| | | | | | |
| | | | | | |
| | | | | | |

### Notes Payable

| Date | Explanation | Ref. | Debit | Credit | Balance |
|---|---|---|---|---|---|
| | | | | | |
| | | | | | |
| | | | | | |

### R. Pitre, Capital

| Date | Explanation | Ref. | Debit | Credit | Balance |
|---|---|---|---|---|---|
| Sept. 1 | Balance | √ | | | 15,700 |
| | | | | | |
| | | | | | |
| | | | | | |

Name: Cumulative Coverage Continued (2)
(a), (c), and (e) (Continued)

### Service Revenue

| Date | Explanation | Ref. | Debit | Credit | Balance |
|------|-------------|------|-------|--------|---------|
|      |             |      |       |        |         |
|      |             |      |       |        |         |
|      |             |      |       |        |         |
|      |             |      |       |        |         |
|      |             |      |       |        |         |
|      |             |      |       |        |         |
|      |             |      |       |        |         |

### Depreciation Expense

| Date | Explanation | Ref. | Debit | Credit | Balance |
|------|-------------|------|-------|--------|---------|
|      |             |      |       |        |         |
|      |             |      |       |        |         |
|      |             |      |       |        |         |
|      |             |      |       |        |         |

### Supplies Expense

| Date | Explanation | Ref. | Debit | Credit | Balance |
|------|-------------|------|-------|--------|---------|
|      |             |      |       |        |         |
|      |             |      |       |        |         |
|      |             |      |       |        |         |
|      |             |      |       |        |         |
|      |             |      |       |        |         |
|      |             |      |       |        |         |

### Salaries Expense

| Date | Explanation | Ref. | Debit | Credit | Balance |
|------|-------------|------|-------|--------|---------|
|      |             |      |       |        |         |
|      |             |      |       |        |         |
|      |             |      |       |        |         |
|      |             |      |       |        |         |
|      |             |      |       |        |         |
|      |             |      |       |        |         |

### Rent Expense

| Date | Explanation | Ref. | Debit | Credit | Balance |
|------|-------------|------|-------|--------|---------|
|      |             |      |       |        |         |
|      |             |      |       |        |         |
|      |             |      |       |        |         |
|      |             |      |       |        |         |

### Interest Expense

| Date | Explanation | Ref. | Debit | Credit | Balance |
|------|-------------|------|-------|--------|---------|
|      |             |      |       |        |         |
|      |             |      |       |        |         |

*Accounting Principles, 5th Canadian Edition*  *Working Papers, Chapter 3*

(b)

## General Journal

| Date | Account Titles and Explanation | Debit | Credit |
|------|-------------------------------|-------|--------|
|      |                               |       |        |

### (e) General Journal

| Date | Account Titles and Explanation | Debit | Credit |
|------|-------------------------------|-------|--------|
|      |                               |       |        |

### (d) and (f)

|  | (d) Unadjusted | | (f) Adjusted | |
|--|----------------|--|--------------|--|
|  | Debit | Credit | Debit | Credit |
|  |       |        |       |        |

(g)

Name            Cumulative Coverage Concluded

**(g) (Continued)**

*Accounting Principles, 5th Canadian Edition*      *Working Papers, Chapter 3*

**Brief Exercise 4-1**

| | |
|---|---|
| 1. | Accounts payable |
| 2. | Accounts receivable |
| 3. | Depreciation expense |
| 4. | General and operating expenses |
| 5. | Property taxes payable |
| 6. | Interest on long-term debt expense |
| 7. | S. Young, capital |
| 8. | Long-term debt |
| 9. | Other revenues |
| 10. | Prepaid expenses |
| 11. | Equipment |
| 12. | S. Young, drawings |
| 13. | Accumulated depreciation |
| 14. | Short-term investments |

Name                                                                                                          Brief Exercise 4-2

(a)                                     General Journal

| Date | Account Titles and Explanation | Debit | Credit |
|------|-------------------------------|-------|--------|
|      |                               |       |        |
|      |                               |       |        |
|      |                               |       |        |
|      |                               |       |        |
|      |                               |       |        |
|      |                               |       |        |
|      |                               |       |        |
|      |                               |       |        |
|      |                               |       |        |
|      |                               |       |        |
|      |                               |       |        |
|      |                               |       |        |
|      |                               |       |        |
|      |                               |       |        |
|      |                               |       |        |
|      |                               |       |        |
|      |                               |       |        |
|      |                               |       |        |
|      |                               |       |        |
|      |                               |       |        |
|      |                               |       |        |
|      |                               |       |        |
|      |                               |       |        |

(b)

*Accounting Principles, 5th Canadian Edition*                                    *Working Papers, Chapter 4*

**Brief Exercise 4-3**

(a)

| General Journal | | | |
|---|---|---|---|
| Date | Account Titles and Explanation | Debit | Credit |
| | | | |
| | | | |
| | | | |
| | | | |
| | | | |
| | | | |
| | | | |
| | | | |
| | | | |
| | | | |
| | | | |
| | | | |
| | | | |
| | | | |
| | | | |
| | | | |

(b)

**BE4-4**

|  | Debit | Credit |
|---|---|---|
|  |  |  |

**BE4-5**

Name          Brief Exercises 4-6 to 4-7

**BE4-6**

(a)

(b)

(c)

(d)

| BE4-7 | Balance Sheet | | | Income Statement | | |
|---|---|---|---|---|---|---|
| | Assets | Liabilities | Owner's Equity | Revenue | Expenses | Profit |
| 1. | U | NE | U | U | NE | U |
| 2. | | | | | | |
| 3. | | | | | | |
| 4. | | | | | | |
| 5. | | | | | | |

Name                                                                        Brief Exercises 4-8 to 4-10

| BE4-8 | General Journal | | |
|---|---|---|---|
| | Account Titles and Explanation | Debit | Credit |
| | | | |
| | | | |
| | | | |
| | | | |
| | | | |
| | | | |
| | | | |
| | | | |
| | | | |
| | | | |
| | | | |
| | | | |
| | | | |
| | | | |
| | | | |
| | | | |
| | | | |
| | | | |
| | | | |
| | | | |

| BE4-9 | # | | | # | |
|---|---|---|---|---|---|
| (a) | | Supplies | (g) | | Unearned Revenue |
| (b) | | Accounts Payable | (h) | | Accounts Receivable |
| (c) | | Building | (i) | | Accumulated Amortization - Bldg |
| (d) | | Prepaid Insurance | (j) | | Patents |
| (e) | | Note Payable (5 Years) | (k) | | Note Receivable (3 Years) |
| (f) | | Goodwill | (l) | | Salaries Payable |

BE4-10

| | |
|---|---|
| | |
| | |
| | |
| | |
| | |
| | |
| | |
| | |
| | |
| | |

*Accounting Principles, 5th Canadian Edition*                                                                        *Working Papers, Chapter 4*

**BE4-11**

**BE4-12**

## *BE4-13

| | Income Statement | | Balance Sheet | |
|---|---|---|---|---|
| | Debit | Credit | Debit | Credit |
| Totals | 37,250 | 28,950 | 37,050 | 45,350 |
| Profit or loss | | | | |
| Totals | | | | |

## *BE4-14

| | Income Statement | | Balance Sheet | |
|---|---|---|---|---|
| | Debit | Credit | Debit | Credit |
| Totals | 33,300 | 45,400 | 71,800 | 59,700 |
| Profit or loss | | | | |
| Totals | | | | |

## *BE4-15

(a) General Journal

| Date | Account Titles and Explanation | Debit | Credit |
|---|---|---|---|
| | | | |

(b) Salaries Expense

| Date | Explanation | Debit | Credit | Balance |
|---|---|---|---|---|
| | | | | |

Salaries Payable

| Date | Explanation | Debit | Credit | Balance |
|---|---|---|---|---|
| | | | | |

Name **Brief Exercise 4-16

**BE4-16

(a) General Journal

| Date | Account Titles and Explanation | Debit | Credit |
|---|---|---|---|
| | | | |

(b) Interest Earned

| Date | Explanation | Debit | Credit | Balance |
|---|---|---|---|---|
| | | | | |

Interest Receivable

| Date | Explanation | Debit | Credit | Balance |
|---|---|---|---|---|
| | | | | |

Name             Exercise 4-1

**E4-1 (a)**

General Journal

| Date | Account Titles and Explanation | Debit | Credit |
|---|---|---|---|
| | | | |

**(b)** Income Summary

| Date | Explanation | Debit | Credit | Balance |
|---|---|---|---|---|
| | | | | |

**(c)**

Name _____   Exercise 4-2

**E4-2(a)**

|  |  |
|---|---|
|  |  |
|  |  |
|  |  |
|  |  |
|  |  |
|  |  |
|  |  |
|  |  |
|  |  |
|  |  |

**E4-2 (b)** General Journal

| Date | Account Titles and Explanation | Debit | Credit |
|---|---|---|---|
|  |  |  |  |
|  |  |  |  |
|  |  |  |  |
|  |  |  |  |
|  |  |  |  |
|  |  |  |  |
|  |  |  |  |
|  |  |  |  |
|  |  |  |  |
|  |  |  |  |

**(b)** Income Summary

| Date | Explanation | Debit | Credit | Balance |
|---|---|---|---|---|
|  |  |  |  |  |
|  |  |  |  |  |
|  |  |  |  |  |
|  |  |  |  |  |
|  |  |  |  |  |

B. Victoire, Drawings

| Date | Explanation | Debit | Credit | Balance |
|---|---|---|---|---|
|  |  |  |  |  |
|  |  |  |  |  |
|  |  |  |  |  |

B. Victoire, Capital

| Date | Explanation | Debit | Credit | Balance |
|---|---|---|---|---|
|  |  |  |  |  |
|  |  |  |  |  |
|  |  |  |  |  |
|  |  |  |  |  |

Accounting Principles, 5th Canadian Edition

Name  Exercise 4-3

**E4-3 (a)**

### General Journal

| Date | Account Titles and Explanation | Debit | Credit |
|---|---|---|---|
| | | | |

### Cash

| Date | Explanation | Ref. | Debit | Credit | Balance |
|---|---|---|---|---|---|
| | | | | | |

### Accounts Receivable

| Date | Explanation | Ref. | Debit | Credit | Balance |
|---|---|---|---|---|---|
| | | | | | |

### Prepaid Expenses

| Date | Explanation | Ref. | Debit | Credit | Balance |
|---|---|---|---|---|---|
| | | | | | |

### Supplies

| Date | Explanation | Ref. | Debit | Credit | Balance |
|---|---|---|---|---|---|
| | | | | | |

*Accounting Principles, 5th Canadian Edition*

Name: _____  Exercise 4-3 Continued (1)

### Equipment

| Date | Explanation | Ref. | Debit | Credit | Balance |
|------|-------------|------|-------|--------|---------|
|      |             |      |       |        |         |
|      |             |      |       |        |         |
|      |             |      |       |        |         |

### Accumulated Amortization-Equipment

| Date | Explanation | Ref. | Debit | Credit | Balance |
|------|-------------|------|-------|--------|---------|
|      |             |      |       |        |         |
|      |             |      |       |        |         |
|      |             |      |       |        |         |

### Accounts Payable

| Date | Explanation | Ref. | Debit | Credit | Balance |
|------|-------------|------|-------|--------|---------|
|      |             |      |       |        |         |
|      |             |      |       |        |         |
|      |             |      |       |        |         |

### Interest Payable

| Date | Explanation | Ref. | Debit | Credit | Balance |
|------|-------------|------|-------|--------|---------|
|      |             |      |       |        |         |
|      |             |      |       |        |         |
|      |             |      |       |        |         |

### Unearned Service Revenue

| Date | Explanation | Ref. | Debit | Credit | Balance |
|------|-------------|------|-------|--------|---------|
|      |             |      |       |        |         |
|      |             |      |       |        |         |
|      |             |      |       |        |         |

### Notes Payable

| Date | Explanation | Ref. | Debit | Credit | Balance |
|------|-------------|------|-------|--------|---------|
|      |             |      |       |        |         |
|      |             |      |       |        |         |
|      |             |      |       |        |         |

### D. Rafael, Capital

| Date | Explanation | Ref. | Debit | Credit | Balance |
|------|-------------|------|-------|--------|---------|
|      |             |      |       |        |         |
|      |             |      |       |        |         |
|      |             |      |       |        |         |
|      |             |      |       |        |         |

### D. Rafael, Drawings

| Date | Explanation | Ref. | Debit | Credit | Balance |
|------|-------------|------|-------|--------|---------|
|      |             |      |       |        |         |
|      |             |      |       |        |         |

Name  Exercise 4-2 Continued (2)

### Service Revenue

| Date | Explanation | Ref. | Debit | Credit | Balance |
|------|-------------|------|-------|--------|---------|
|      |             |      |       |        |         |
|      |             |      |       |        |         |
|      |             |      |       |        |         |

### Depreciation Expense

| Date | Explanation | Ref. | Debit | Credit | Balance |
|------|-------------|------|-------|--------|---------|
|      |             |      |       |        |         |
|      |             |      |       |        |         |
|      |             |      |       |        |         |

### Salaries Expense

| Date | Explanation | Ref. | Debit | Credit | Balance |
|------|-------------|------|-------|--------|---------|
|      |             |      |       |        |         |
|      |             |      |       |        |         |
|      |             |      |       |        |         |
|      |             |      |       |        |         |

### Interest Expense

| Date | Explanation | Ref. | Debit | Credit | Balance |
|------|-------------|------|-------|--------|---------|
|      |             |      |       |        |         |
|      |             |      |       |        |         |
|      |             |      |       |        |         |

### Rent Expense

| Date | Explanation | Ref. | Debit | Credit | Balance |
|------|-------------|------|-------|--------|---------|
|      |             |      |       |        |         |
|      |             |      |       |        |         |
|      |             |      |       |        |         |

### Supplies Expense

| Date | Explanation | Ref. | Debit | Credit | Balance |
|------|-------------|------|-------|--------|---------|
|      |             |      |       |        |         |
|      |             |      |       |        |         |
|      |             |      |       |        |         |

### Income Summary

| Date | Explanation | Ref. | Debit | Credit | Balance |
|------|-------------|------|-------|--------|---------|
|      |             |      |       |        |         |
|      |             |      |       |        |         |
|      |             |      |       |        |         |
|      |             |      |       |        |         |

(b)

|  | Debit | Credit |
|---|---|---|
|  |  |  |

Name  Exercise 4-4

**(a)**

### General Journal

| Date | Account Titles and Explanation | Debit | Credit |
|------|-------------------------------|-------|--------|
|      |                               |       |        |
|      |                               |       |        |
|      |                               |       |        |
|      |                               |       |        |
|      |                               |       |        |
|      |                               |       |        |
|      |                               |       |        |
|      |                               |       |        |
|      |                               |       |        |
|      |                               |       |        |
|      |                               |       |        |
|      |                               |       |        |
|      |                               |       |        |
|      |                               |       |        |
|      |                               |       |        |
|      |                               |       |        |
|      |                               |       |        |
|      |                               |       |        |

**(b)**

E4-4 (c)

| | Debit | Credit |
|---|---|---|
| | | |

Name                                                                                         Exercise 4-5

(a)                              General Journal

| Date | Account Titles and Explanation | Debit | Credit |
|------|-------------------------------|-------|--------|
|      |                               |       |        |
|      |                               |       |        |
|      |                               |       |        |
|      |                               |       |        |
|      |                               |       |        |
|      |                               |       |        |
|      |                               |       |        |
|      |                               |       |        |
|      |                               |       |        |
|      |                               |       |        |
|      |                               |       |        |
|      |                               |       |        |
|      |                               |       |        |
|      |                               |       |        |
|      |                               |       |        |

(b)(c)and(e)

*Accounting Principles, 5th Canadian Edition*                              *Working Papers, Chapter 4*

**Exercise 4-5 Concluded**

**E4-5 (c)**                       General Journal

| Date | Account Titles and Explanation | Debit | Credit |
|---|---|---|---|
| | | | |
| | | | |
| | | | |
| | | | |
| | | | |
| | | | |
| | | | |
| | | | |
| | | | |
| | | | |
| | | | |

**E4-5(d)**

| | Debit | Credit |
|---|---|---|
| | | |
| | | |
| | | |
| | | |
| | | |
| | | |
| | | |
| | | |
| | | |
| | | |
| | | |
| | | |
| | | |

**E4-5 (e)**                       General Journal

| Date | Account Titles and Explanation | Debit | Credit |
|---|---|---|---|
| | | | |
| | | | |
| | | | |
| | | | |
| | | | |
| | | | |
| | | | |
| | | | |
| | | | |
| | | | |
| | | | |
| | | | |

Name  Exercise 4-6

### E4-6(a) General Journal

| Date | Account Titles and Explanation | Debit | Credit |
|---|---|---|---|
| | | | |

### (b)

| Error | Balance Sheet | | | Income Statement | | |
|---|---|---|---|---|---|---|
| | Assets | Liabilities | Owner's Equity | Revenue | Expenses | Profit |
| 1. | O | O | NE | NE | NE | NE |
| 2. | | | | | | |
| 3. | | | | | | |
| 4. | | | | | | |
| 5. | | | | | | |

## E4-7(a) and (b) — General Journal

| | Account Titles and Explanation | Debit | Credit |
|---|---|---|---|
| | | | |

Name | Exercise 4-8

| Account | (a) B/S or I/S | (b) Balance Sheet Classification |
|---|---|---|
| Accounts payable and accrued liabilities | | |
| Accounts receivable | | |
| Accumulated other comprehensive loss | | |
| Capital assets | | |
| Capital stock | | |
| Cash and cash equivalents | | |
| Contributed surplus | | |
| Current portion of long-term debt | | |
| Employee future benefit obligation | | |
| Financing expenses | | |
| General and operating expenses | | |
| Goodwill | | |
| Income tax expense | | |
| Income taxes payable | | |
| Income taxes receivable | | |
| Inventories | | |
| Investments | | |
| Long-term debt | | |
| Long-term debt due within one year | | |
| Long-term lease obligation | | |
| Mortgages and loans receivable | | |
| Other revenues | | |
| Prepaid expenses | | |
| Retained earnings | | |

*Accounting Principles, 5th Canadian Edition* — *Working Papers, Chapter 4*

E4-9 (a)

(b)

Name  Exercise 4-10

(a)

(b)

(c)

**(a) (Continued)**

*Exercise 4-12

GARDENS DESIGNS
Work Sheet
Month Ended April 30, 2011

| Account Titles | Unadjusted Trial Balance | | Adjustments | | Adjusted Trial Balance | | Income Statement | | Balance Sheet | |
|---|---|---|---|---|---|---|---|---|---|---|
| | Dr. | Cr. | Dr. | Cr. | Dr. | Cr. | Dr. | Cr. | Dr. | Cr. |
| Cash | 14,840 | | | | | | | | | |
| Accounts receivable | 8,780 | | | | | | | | | |
| Prepaid rent | 4,875 | | | | | | | | | |
| Equipment | 18,900 | | | | | | | | | |
| Accumulated depreciation-equipment | | 4,725 | | | | | | | | |
| Accounts payable | | 5,670 | | | | | | | | |
| Notes payable | | 11,600 | | | | | | | | |
| Interest payable | | | | | | | | | | |
| T.Hibbiscus, capital | | 25,960 | | | | | | | | |
| T.Hibbiscus, drawings | 3,650 | | | | | | | | | |
| Service revenue | | 12,930 | | | | | | | | | |
| Salaries expense | 9,840 | | | | | | | | | |
| Rent expense | | | | | | | | | | |
| Depreciation expense | | | | | | | | | | |
| Interest expense | | | | | | | | | | |
| Totals | 60,885 | 60,885 | | | | | | | | |
| Profit | | | | | | | | | | |
| Totals | | | | | | | | | | |

Name *Exercise 4-13

(a), (b), and (c)

## General Journal

| Date | Account Titles and Explanation | Debit | Credit |
|------|-------------------------------|-------|--------|
|      |                               |       |        |

## Income Summary

| Date | Explanation | Debit | Credit | Balance |
|------|-------------|-------|--------|---------|
|      |             |       |        |         |

Name  *Exercise 4-13 Continued (1)

(a), (b) and (c) (Continued)     Cash

| Date | Explanation | Ref. | Debit | Credit | Balance |
|---|---|---|---|---|---|
| | | | | | |
| | | | | | |
| | | | | | |

Accounts Receivable

| Date | Explanation | Ref. | Debit | Credit | Balance |
|---|---|---|---|---|---|
| | | | | | |
| | | | | | |
| | | | | | |
| | | | | | |

Interest Payable

| Date | Explanation | Ref. | Debit | Credit | Balance |
|---|---|---|---|---|---|
| | | | | | |
| | | | | | |
| | | | | | |
| | | | | | |

I. Masterson, Capital

| Date | Explanation | Ref. | Debit | Credit | Balance |
|---|---|---|---|---|---|
| | | | | | |
| | | | | | |
| | | | | | |

Commission Revenue

| Date | Explanation | Ref. | Debit | Credit | Balance |
|---|---|---|---|---|---|
| | | | | | |
| | | | | | |
| | | | | | |
| | | | | | |
| | | | | | |
| | | | | | |
| | | | | | |

Interest Expense

| Date | Explanation | Ref. | Debit | Credit | Balance |
|---|---|---|---|---|---|
| | | | | | |
| | | | | | |
| | | | | | |
| | | | | | |
| | | | | | |
| | | | | | |

Name *Exercise 4-14

**\*E4-14 (a)**

**(b)** General Journal

| Date | Account Titles and Explanation | Debit | Credit |
|------|-------------------------------|-------|--------|
|      |                               |       |        |
|      |                               |       |        |
|      |                               |       |        |
|      |                               |       |        |
|      |                               |       |        |
|      |                               |       |        |
|      |                               |       |        |
|      |                               |       |        |
|      |                               |       |        |
|      |                               |       |        |
|      |                               |       |        |
|      |                               |       |        |
|      |                               |       |        |
|      |                               |       |        |
|      |                               |       |        |
|      |                               |       |        |
|      |                               |       |        |
|      |                               |       |        |

**(c)**

Name  Problem 4-1A

**(b)**

## General Journal

| Date | Account Titles and Explanation | Debit | Credit |
|---|---|---|---|
| | | | |

**(b)** Income Summary

Problem 4-1A Concluded

(c)

|  | Debit | Credit |
|---|---|---|
|  |  |  |
|  |  |  |
|  |  |  |
|  |  |  |
|  |  |  |
|  |  |  |
|  |  |  |

(d)

*Taking It Further*

Name    Problem 4-2A

(a)

(a) (Continued)

(b)

## General Journal

| Date | Account Titles and Explanation | Debit | Credit |
|------|-------------------------------|-------|--------|
|      |                               |       |        |

(c)

Income Summary

**Problem 4-2A Concluded**

(d)

|  | Debit | Credit |
|---|---|---|
|  |  |  |
|  |  |  |
|  |  |  |
|  |  |  |
|  |  |  |
|  |  |  |
|  |  |  |
|  |  |  |
|  |  |  |
|  |  |  |
|  |  |  |
|  |  |  |
|  |  |  |
|  |  |  |
|  |  |  |
|  |  |  |
|  |  |  |
|  |  |  |
|  |  |  |
|  |  |  |
|  |  |  |
|  |  |  |
|  |  |  |

*Taking It Further*

Name	Problem 4-3A

(a)

## General Journal

| Date | Account Titles and Explanation | Debit | Credit |
|---|---|---|---|
| | | | |

(b)

|  | Debit | Credit |
|---|---|---|
|  |  |  |

(c)

**(c) (Continued)**

**Problem 4-3A Concluded**

(d)

## General Journal

| Date | Account Titles and Explanation | Debit | Credit |
|------|-------------------------------|-------|--------|
|      |                               |       |        |

**Taking It Further**

Problem 4-4A

**(a)**

### General Journal

| Date | Account Titles and Explanation | Debit | Credit |
|------|-------------------------------|-------|--------|
|      |                               |       |        |

Name                                                                           Problem 4-4 Continued (1)

(a), (c) and (f) (Continued)

### Cash

| Date | Explanation | Ref. | Debit | Credit | Balance |
|------|-------------|------|-------|--------|---------|
|      |             |      |       |        |         |
|      |             |      |       |        |         |
|      |             |      |       |        |         |
|      |             |      |       |        |         |
|      |             |      |       |        |         |
|      |             |      |       |        |         |
|      |             |      |       |        |         |
|      |             |      |       |        |         |
|      |             |      |       |        |         |
|      |             |      |       |        |         |

### Accounts Receivable

| Date | Explanation | Ref. | Debit | Credit | Balance |
|------|-------------|------|-------|--------|---------|
|      |             |      |       |        |         |
|      |             |      |       |        |         |
|      |             |      |       |        |         |
|      |             |      |       |        |         |
|      |             |      |       |        |         |

### Cleaning Supplies

| Date | Explanation | Ref. | Debit | Credit | Balance |
|------|-------------|------|-------|--------|---------|
|      |             |      |       |        |         |
|      |             |      |       |        |         |
|      |             |      |       |        |         |
|      |             |      |       |        |         |

### Prepaid Insurance

| Date | Explanation | Ref. | Debit | Credit | Balance |
|------|-------------|------|-------|--------|---------|
|      |             |      |       |        |         |
|      |             |      |       |        |         |
|      |             |      |       |        |         |

### Equipment

| Date | Explanation | Ref. | Debit | Credit | Balance |
|------|-------------|------|-------|--------|---------|
|      |             |      |       |        |         |
|      |             |      |       |        |         |
|      |             |      |       |        |         |

### Accumulated Depreciation - Equipment

| Date | Explanation | Ref. | Debit | Credit | Balance |
|------|-------------|------|-------|--------|---------|
|      |             |      |       |        |         |
|      |             |      |       |        |         |
|      |             |      |       |        |         |

Name                                                                 Problem 4-4 Continued (2)

(a), (c) and (f) (Continued)

### Accounts Payable

| Date | Explanation | Ref. | Debit | Credit | Balance |
|------|-------------|------|-------|--------|---------|
|      |             |      |       |        |         |
|      |             |      |       |        |         |
|      |             |      |       |        |         |

### Salaries Payable

| Date | Explanation | Ref. | Debit | Credit | Balance |
|------|-------------|------|-------|--------|---------|
|      |             |      |       |        |         |
|      |             |      |       |        |         |
|      |             |      |       |        |         |

### Interest Payable

| Date | Explanation | Ref. | Debit | Credit | Balance |
|------|-------------|------|-------|--------|---------|
|      |             |      |       |        |         |
|      |             |      |       |        |         |
|      |             |      |       |        |         |

### Note Payable

| Date | Explanation | Ref. | Debit | Credit | Balance |
|------|-------------|------|-------|--------|---------|
|      |             |      |       |        |         |
|      |             |      |       |        |         |
|      |             |      |       |        |         |

### L. Chang, Capital

| Date | Explanation | Ref. | Debit | Credit | Balance |
|------|-------------|------|-------|--------|---------|
|      |             |      |       |        |         |
|      |             |      |       |        |         |
|      |             |      |       |        |         |
|      |             |      |       |        |         |
|      |             |      |       |        |         |

### L. Chang, Drawings

| Date | Explanation | Ref. | Debit | Credit | Balance |
|------|-------------|------|-------|--------|---------|
|      |             |      |       |        |         |
|      |             |      |       |        |         |
|      |             |      |       |        |         |
|      |             |      |       |        |         |

### Income Summary

| Date | Explanation | Ref. | Debit | Credit | Balance |
|------|-------------|------|-------|--------|---------|
|      |             |      |       |        |         |
|      |             |      |       |        |         |
|      |             |      |       |        |         |
|      |             |      |       |        |         |

Name  Problem 4-4 Continued (3)

(a), (c) and (f) (Continued)

### Cleaning Revenue

| Date | Explanation | Ref. | Debit | Credit | Balance |
|------|-------------|------|-------|--------|---------|
|      |             |      |       |        |         |
|      |             |      |       |        |         |
|      |             |      |       |        |         |
|      |             |      |       |        |         |
|      |             |      |       |        |         |
|      |             |      |       |        |         |

### Gas & Oil Expenses

| Date | Explanation | Ref. | Debit | Credit | Balance |
|------|-------------|------|-------|--------|---------|
|      |             |      |       |        |         |
|      |             |      |       |        |         |
|      |             |      |       |        |         |

### Salaries Expense

| Date | Explanation | Ref. | Debit | Credit | Balance |
|------|-------------|------|-------|--------|---------|
|      |             |      |       |        |         |
|      |             |      |       |        |         |
|      |             |      |       |        |         |
|      |             |      |       |        |         |
|      |             |      |       |        |         |

### Cleaning Supplies Expense

| Date | Explanation | Ref. | Debit | Credit | Balance |
|------|-------------|------|-------|--------|---------|
|      |             |      |       |        |         |
|      |             |      |       |        |         |
|      |             |      |       |        |         |

### Depreciation Expense

| Date | Explanation | Ref. | Debit | Credit | Balance |
|------|-------------|------|-------|--------|---------|
|      |             |      |       |        |         |
|      |             |      |       |        |         |
|      |             |      |       |        |         |

### Insurance Expense

| Date | Explanation | Ref. | Debit | Credit | Balance |
|------|-------------|------|-------|--------|---------|
|      |             |      |       |        |         |
|      |             |      |       |        |         |
|      |             |      |       |        |         |

### Interest Expense

| Date | Explanation | Ref. | Debit | Credit | Balance |
|------|-------------|------|-------|--------|---------|
|      |             |      |       |        |         |
|      |             |      |       |        |         |
|      |             |      |       |        |         |

(b)

|  | Debit | Credit |
|---|---|---|
|  |  |  |

(c) General Journal

| Date | Account Titles and Explanation | Debit | Credit |
|---|---|---|---|
|  |  |  |  |

(d)

|  | Debit | Credit |
|---|---|---|
|  |  |  |

(e)

(e) (Continued)

**Problem 4-4A Concluded**

(f)

### General Journal

| Date | Account Titles and Explanation | Debit | Credit |
|------|-------------------------------|-------|--------|
|      |                               |       |        |

(g)

|  | Debit | Credit |
|--|-------|--------|
|  |       |        |

*Taking It Further*

Problem 4-5A

(a)

| (1) Incorrect Entry | | | (2) Correct Entry | | | (3) Correcting Entry | | |
|---|---|---|---|---|---|---|---|---|
| | | | | | | | | |

(b)

|  | Debit | Credit |
|---|---|---|
|  |  |  |

**Taking It Further**

Name | Problem 4-6A

## (a)

| Item | Income Statement | | | Balance Sheet | | |
|---|---|---|---|---|---|---|
| | Revenue | Expenses | Profit | Assets | Liabilities | Owner's Equity |
| 1. | NE | U $500 | O $500 | NE | U $500 | O $500 |
| 2. | | | | | | |
| 3. | | | | | | |
| 4. | | | | | | |
| 5. | | | | | | |
| 6. | | | | | | |
| 7. | | | | | | |
| 8. | | | | | | |

## (b)

| General Journal | | |
|---|---|---|
| Account Titles and Explanation | Debit | Credit |
| | | |

Accounting Principles, 5th Canadian Edition — Working Papers, Chapter 4

**Problem 4-6A Concluded**

(b)

### General Journal

| | | Account Titles and Explanation | Debit | Credit |
|---|---|---|---|---|

**Taking It Further**

**Problem 4-7A**

(a) Although not required, the closing entries would be:

| (a) | General Journal | | |
|---|---|---|---|
| | Account Titles and Explanation | Debit | Credit |
| | | | |

**F. Dunder, Capital**

(b)

| (c) | December 31, 2011 | December 31, 2010 |
|---|---|---|
| Working Capital | | |
| Current Ratio | | |

| (d) | December 31, 2011 | December 31, 2010 |
|---|---|---|
| Acid-test Ratio | | |

*Taking It Further*

Name  Problem 4-8A

**P4-8A (a)**

|  | 2009 | 2008 | 2007 |
|---|---|---|---|
| Working Capital |  |  |  |
| Current Ratio |  |  |  |
| Acid-test Ratio |  |  |  |

**(b)**

**Taking It Further**

# Elbow Cycle Repair Shop
## Work Sheet
### Year Ended January 31, 2011

| Account Titles | Trial Balance Dr. | Trial Balance Cr. | Adjustments Dr. | Adjustments Cr. | Adjusted Trial Balance Dr. | Adjusted Trial Balance Cr. | Income Statement Dr. | Income Statement Cr. | Balance Sheet Dr. | Balance Sheet Cr. |
|---|---|---|---|---|---|---|---|---|---|---|
| Cash | 3,200 | | | | | | | | | |
| Accounts receivable | 6,630 | | | | | | | | | |
| Prepaid insurance | 6,420 | | | | | | | | | |
| Supplies | 5,240 | | | | | | | | | |
| Land | 50,000 | | | | | | | | | |
| Building | 90,000 | | | | | | | | | |
| Accum. deprec. - building | | 11,000 | | | | | | | | |
| Equipment | 27,000 | | | | | | | | | |
| Accum. deprec. - equip. | | 4,500 | | | | | | | | |
| Accounts payable | | 6,400 | | | | | | | | |
| Salaries payable | | | | | | | | | | |
| Salaries payable | | | | | | | | | | |
| Interest payable | | | | | | | | | | |
| Unearned revenue | | 1,950 | | | | | | | | |
| Mortgage payable | | 102,000 | | | | | | | | |
| H. Dude, capital | | 61,000 | | | | | | | | |
| H. Dude, drawings | 101,100 | | | | | | | | | |
| Service revenue | | 235,550 | | | | | | | | |
| Salaries expense | 115,200 | | | | | | | | | |
| Utilities expense | 12,000 | | | | | | | | | |
| Interest expense | 5,610 | | | | | | | | | |
| Insurance expense | | | | | | | | | | |
| Supplies expense | | | | | | | | | | |
| Depreciation expense | | | | | | | | | | |
| Totals | 422,400 | 422,400 | | | | | | | | |
| Profit | | | | | | | | | | |
| Totals | | | | | | | | | | |

Taking It Further

*Problem 4-10A

(a)

# WATER WORLD PARK
## Work Sheet
### Year Ended September 30, 2011

| Account Titles | Trial Balance Dr. | Trial Balance Cr. | Adjustments Dr. | Adjustments Cr. | Adjusted Trial Balance Dr. | Adjusted Trial Balance Cr. | Income Statement Dr. | Income Statement Cr. | Balance Sheet Dr. | Balance Sheet Cr. |
|---|---|---|---|---|---|---|---|---|---|---|
| Cash | 11,770 | | | | | | | | | |
| Accounts receivable | | | | | | | | | | |
| Supplies | 18,600 | | | | | | | | | |
| Prepaid insurance | 33,000 | | | | | | | | | |
| Land | 80,000 | | | | | | | | | |
| Building | 480,000 | | | | | | | | | |
| Accum. Deprec. - bldg. | | 96,000 | | | | | | | | |
| Equipment | 120,000 | | | | | | | | | |
| Accum. deprec. - equip. | | 48,000 | | | | | | | | |
| Accounts payable | | 23,600 | | | | | | | | |
| Wages payable | | | | | | | | | | |
| Interest payable | | | | | | | | | | |
| Unearned adm. revenue | | 3,700 | | | | | | | | |
| Mortgage payable | | 350,000 | | | | | | | | |
| M. Berge, capital | | 175,450 | | | | | | | | |
| M. Berge, drawings | 14,000 | | | | | | | | | |
| Admission revenue | | 250,065 | | | | | | | | |
| Concession revenue | | 16,720 | | | | | | | | |
| Wages expense | 123,000 | | | | | | | | | |
| Repairs expense | 30,500 | | | | | | | | | |
| Advertising expense | 9,660 | | | | | | | | | |
| Utilities expense | 16,900 | | | | | | | | | |
| Insurance expense | 5500 | | | | | | | | | |
| Interest expense | 20,605 | | | | | | | | | |
| Depreciation expense | | | | | | | | | | |
| Supplies expense | | | | | | | | | | |
| Totals | 963,535 | 963,535 | | | | | | | | |
| Loss | | | | | | | | | | |
| Totals | | | | | | | | | | |

(b)

**(c) and (d)**

### General Journal

| Date | Account Titles and Explanation | Debit | Credit |
|------|-------------------------------|-------|--------|
|      |                               |       |        |

**Problem 4-10A Concluded**

(e)

|  | Debit | Credit |
|---|---|---|
|  |  |  |

*Taking It Further*

*P4-11A (a) 1.

## General Journal

| Date | Account Titles and Explanation | Debit | Credit |
|------|-------------------------------|-------|--------|
|      |                               |       |        |

**(a) (Continued)**

2.

| Interest Receivable | Interest Revenue |
|---|---|
| | |

| Wages Payable | Wages Expense |
|---|---|
| | |

| Prepaid Insurance | Insurance Expense |
|---|---|
| | |

| Unearned Service Revenue | Service Revenue |
|---|---|
| | |

(b) 1. and 2.

## General Journal

| Date | Account Titles and Explanation | Debit | Credit |
|------|-------------------------------|-------|--------|
|      |                               |       |        |

**Problem 4-11A Concluded**

(b) (Continued)

3.

| Interest Receivable | Interest Revenue |
|---|---|

| Wages Payable | Wages Expense |
|---|---|

| Prepaid Insurance | Insurance Expense |
|---|---|

| Unearned Service Revenue | Service Revenue |
|---|---|

(c)

*Taking It Further*

# General Journal

| Date | Account Titles and Explanation | Debit | Credit |
|------|-------------------------------|-------|--------|
|      |                               |       |        |

*Problem 4-12A Concluded

| General Journal | | | |
|---|---|---|---|
| Date | Account Titles and Explanation | Debit | Credit |
| | | | |

**Taking It Further**

(a)

(a) (Continued)

Name                                                                 Continuing Cookie Chronicle Concluded

**(b)**                         General Journal

| Date | Account Titles and Explanation | Debit | Credit |
|------|-------------------------------|-------|--------|
|      |                               |       |        |
|      |                               |       |        |
|      |                               |       |        |

**(c)**

|  | Debit | Credit |
|--|-------|--------|
|  |       |        |
|  |       |        |
|  |       |        |

(b)

## General Journal

| Date | Account Titles and Explanation | Debit | Credit |
|------|-------------------------------|-------|--------|
|      |                               |       |        |

(a),(c),(e) and (h)

| Cash | Accounts Receivable |
|---|---|
| | |

| | Supplies |
|---|---|
| | |

| Equipment | Accumulated Depreciation-Equipment |
|---|---|
| | |

| Accounts Payable | Unearned Service Revenue |
|---|---|
| | |

| Salaries Payable | Interest Payable |
|---|---|
| | |

(a),(c),(e) and (h)

| Note Payable | J. Alou, Capital |
|---|---|
| | |

| J. Alou, Drawings | Income Summary |
|---|---|
| | |

| Service Revenue | Rent Expense |
|---|---|
| | |

| Salaries Expense | Telephone Expense |
|---|---|
| | |

| Supplies Expense | Depreciation Expense |
|---|---|
| | |

| Interest Expense | |
|---|---|
| | |

(d)

|  | Debit | Credit |
|---|---|---|
|  |  |  |

(e)

## General Journal

| Date | Account Titles and Explanation | Debit | Credit |
|------|-------------------------------|-------|--------|
|      |                               |       |        |

(f)

(g)

**(g)(Continued)**

## (h)

### General Journal

| Date | Account Titles and Explanation | Debit | Credit |
|------|-------------------------------|-------|--------|
|      |                               |       |        |
|      |                               |       |        |
|      |                               |       |        |
|      |                               |       |        |
|      |                               |       |        |
|      |                               |       |        |
|      |                               |       |        |
|      |                               |       |        |
|      |                               |       |        |
|      |                               |       |        |
|      |                               |       |        |
|      |                               |       |        |
|      |                               |       |        |
|      |                               |       |        |
|      |                               |       |        |
|      |                               |       |        |
|      |                               |       |        |
|      |                               |       |        |
|      |                               |       |        |
|      |                               |       |        |

## (i)

|   | Debit | Credit |
|---|-------|--------|
|   |       |        |
|   |       |        |
|   |       |        |
|   |       |        |
|   |       |        |
|   |       |        |
|   |       |        |
|   |       |        |
|   |       |        |
|   |       |        |
|   |       |        |
|   |       |        |
|   |       |        |
|   |       |        |
|   |       |        |
|   |       |        |
|   |       |        |
|   |       |        |

**BE5-1**

**BE5-2**

**BE5-3**

Name  Brief Exercises 5-4 to 5-6

| BE5-4 Date | Assets | Liabilities | Owner's Equity | Revenue | Expenses | Profit |
|---|---|---|---|---|---|---|
| Feb. 5 | Inventory + 10,000 | Accounts Payable + 10,000 | NE | | | NE |
| 6 | | | | | | |
| 8 | | | | | | |
| 11 | | | | | | |

**BE5-5** General Journal

| Date | Account Titles and Explanation | Debit | Credit |
|---|---|---|---|
| | | | |
| | | | |
| | | | |
| | | | |
| | | | |
| | | | |
| | | | |
| | | | |
| | | | |
| | | | |
| | | | |
| | | | |
| | | | |
| | | | |

**BE5-6** General Journal

| Date | Account Titles and Explanation | Debit | Credit |
|---|---|---|---|
| | | | |
| | | | |
| | | | |
| | | | |
| | | | |
| | | | |
| | | | |
| | | | |
| | | | |
| | | | |
| | | | |
| | | | |
| | | | |
| | | | |
| | | | |

*Accounting Principles, 5th Canadian Edition*  *Working Papers, Chapter 5*

## Brief Exercise 5-7

| Date | Assets | Liabilities | Owner's Equity | Revenue | Expenses | Profit |
|------|--------|-------------|----------------|---------|----------|--------|
|      |        |             |                |         |          |        |
|      |        |             |                |         |          |        |
|      |        |             |                |         |          |        |
|      |        |             |                |         |          |        |
|      |        |             |                |         |          |        |
|      |        |             |                |         |          |        |

**Name** — Brief Exercises 5-8 to 5-9

**BE5-8**     General Journal

| Date | Account Titles and Explanation | Debit | Credit |
|------|-------------------------------|-------|--------|
|      |                               |       |        |
|      |                               |       |        |
|      |                               |       |        |
|      |                               |       |        |
|      |                               |       |        |
|      |                               |       |        |
|      |                               |       |        |
|      |                               |       |        |
|      |                               |       |        |
|      |                               |       |        |
|      |                               |       |        |
|      |                               |       |        |
|      |                               |       |        |
|      |                               |       |        |
|      |                               |       |        |
|      |                               |       |        |
|      |                               |       |        |
|      |                               |       |        |
|      |                               |       |        |

**BE5-9**     General Journal

| Date | Account Titles and Explanation | Debit | Credit |
|------|-------------------------------|-------|--------|
|      |                               |       |        |
|      |                               |       |        |
|      |                               |       |        |
|      |                               |       |        |
|      |                               |       |        |
|      |                               |       |        |
|      |                               |       |        |
|      |                               |       |        |
|      |                               |       |        |
|      |                               |       |        |
|      |                               |       |        |
|      |                               |       |        |
|      |                               |       |        |
|      |                               |       |        |
|      |                               |       |        |
|      |                               |       |        |
|      |                               |       |        |
|      |                               |       |        |
|      |                               |       |        |

*Accounting Principles, 5th Canadian Edition*     *Working Papers, Chapter 5*

**BE5-10**

| Date | General Journal<br>Account Titles and Explanation | Debit | Credit |
|------|---------------------------------------------------|-------|--------|
|      |                                                   |       |        |
|      |                                                   |       |        |
|      |                                                   |       |        |
|      |                                                   |       |        |
|      |                                                   |       |        |

**BE5-11**

| Date | General Journal<br>Account Titles and Explanation | Debit | Credit |
|------|---------------------------------------------------|-------|--------|
|      |                                                   |       |        |
|      |                                                   |       |        |
|      |                                                   |       |        |
|      |                                                   |       |        |
|      |                                                   |       |        |
|      |                                                   |       |        |
|      |                                                   |       |        |
|      |                                                   |       |        |
|      |                                                   |       |        |
|      |                                                   |       |        |

**BE5-12**

# BE5-13

| | (a) Single-step income statement | (b) Multiple-step income statement |
|---|---|---|
| | | |
| | | |
| | | |
| | | |
| | | |
| | | |
| | | |
| | | |
| | | |
| | | |
| | | |
| | | |

# BE5-14

| | 2010 | 2011 |
|---|---|---|
| Gross profit margin | | |
| | | |
| Profit margin | | |
| | | |
| | | |
| | | |
| | | |

# *BE5-15

General Journal

| Date | Account Titles and Explanation | Debit | Credit |
|---|---|---|---|
| | | | |
| | | | |
| | | | |
| | | | |
| | | | |
| | | | |
| | | | |
| | | | |
| | | | |
| | | | |
| | | | |
| | | | |

**Brief Exercises 5-16 to 5-17**

***BE5-16**

### General Journal

| Date | Account Titles and Explanation | Debit | Credit |
|------|-------------------------------|-------|--------|
|      |                               |       |        |

***BE5-17**

Name — Exercises 5-1 and 5-3

| E5-1 | |
|---|---|
| (a) | |
| (b) | |
| (c) | |
| (d) | |
| (e) | |
| (f) | |
| (g) | |
| (h) | |
| (i) | |
| (j) | |
| (k) | |
| (l) | |
| (m) | |
| (n) | |

E5-3 General Journal

| Date | Account Titles and Explanation | Debit | Credit |
|---|---|---|---|
| | | | |

Exercise 5-2

## Balance Sheet

| Inventory Transaction | Type of Account | Account Name | Increase or Decrease | Impact on Owner's Equity |
|---|---|---|---|---|
| 1. | Asset<br>Liability | Inventory<br>Accounts Payable | Increase<br>Increase | NE |
| 2. | | | | |
| 3. | | | | |
| 4. | | | | |
| 5. | | | | |
| 6. | | | | |
| 7. | | | | |
| 8. | | | | |

## Income Statement

| Inventory Transaction | Type of Account | Account Name | Increase or Decrease | Impact on Profit |
|---|---|---|---|---|
| 1. | NE | | | NE |
| 2. | | | | |
| 3. | | | | |
| 4. | | | | |
| 5. | | | | |
| 6. | | | | |
| 7. | | | | |
| 8. | | | | |

Name — Exercise 5-4

## General Journal

| Date | Account Titles and Explanation | Debit | Credit |
|------|-------------------------------|-------|--------|
|      |                               |       |        |

## (c) General Journal

| Date | Account Titles and Explanation | Debit | Credit |
|------|-------------------------------|-------|--------|
|      |                               |       |        |

Exercise 5-9

| Account | Statement | Classification |
|---|---|---|
| Accounts Payable | Balance Sheet | Current Liabilities |
| Accounts Receivable | | |
| Accumulated Depreciation - Office Building | | |
| Advertising Expense | | |
| Depreciation Expense | | |
| B. Swirsky, Capital | | |
| B. Swirsky, Drawings | | |
| Cash | | |
| Freight Out | | |
| Insurance Expense | | |
| Interest Expense | | |
| Interest Payable | | |
| Interest Revenue | | |
| Land | | |
| Merchandise Inventory | | |
| Mortgage Payable | | |
| Note Receivable (6 months) | | |
| Office Building | | |
| Prepaid Insurance | | |
| Property Tax Payable | | |
| Salaries Expense | | |
| Salaries Payable | | |
| Sales | | |
| Sales Discounts | | |
| Sales Returns and Allowances | | |
| Unearned Sales Revenue | | |

Exercise 5-10

(a)

**Exercise 5-10 Concluded**

(a)

(b)

*Exercise 5-12

## General Journal

| Date | Account Titles and Explanation | Debit | Credit |
|------|-------------------------------|-------|--------|
|      |                               |       |        |

*Exercise 5-13

(a)

**General Journal**

| Date | Account Titles and Explanation | Debit | Credit |
|------|-------------------------------|-------|--------|
|      |                               |       |        |

**(b)** General Journal

| Date | Account Titles and Explanation | Debit | Credit |
|------|-------------------------------|-------|--------|
|      |                               |       |        |

Name *Exercise 5-14

**(a)** General Journal

| Date | Account Titles and Explanation | Debit | Credit |
|------|-------------------------------|-------|--------|
|      |                               |       |        |

**(b)**

|  |  |  |
|--|--|--|
|  |  |  |

Name  *Exercise 5-15

**Company 1**

(a)
(b)
(c)
(d)
(e)
(f)
(g)
(h)
(i)

**Company 2**

(j)
(k)
(l)
(m)
(n)
(o)
(p)
(q)
(r)

*Exercise 5-16

(a)

*Exercise 5-16 Concluded

**(b) General Journal**

| Date | Account Titles and Explanation | Debit | Credit |
|------|-------------------------------|-------|--------|
|      |                               |       |        |

Problem 5-1A

*Taking It Further*

## (a) General Journal

| Date | Account Titles and Explanation | Debit | Credit |
|------|-------------------------------|-------|--------|
|      |                               |       |        |

Name | Problem 5-2A Concluded

**(b)**

| Inventory | Cost of Goods Sold |
|---|---|
| | |

| Sales | Sales Returns and Allowances |
|---|---|
| | |

**(c)**

*Taking It Further*

**(a)** General Journal

| Date | Account Titles and Explanation | Debit | Credit |
|---|---|---|---|
| | | | |

**(b)**

Merchandise Inventory

**(c)**

*Taking It Further*

Problem 5-4A

| General Journal | | | |
|---|---|---|---|
| Date | Account Titles and Explanation | Debit | Credit |
| | | | |

Problem 5-4A Concluded

## General Journal

| Date | Account Titles and Explanation | Debit | Credit |
|------|-------------------------------|-------|--------|
|      |                               |       |        |

*Taking It Further*

Problem 5-5A

(a) General Journal

| Date | Account Titles and Explanation | Debit | Credit |
|------|-------------------------------|-------|--------|
|      |                               |       |        |

**(a) (Continued)**

## General Journal

| Date | Account Titles and Explanation | Debit | Credit |
|------|-------------------------------|-------|--------|
|      |                               |       |        |

Problem 5-5A Continued (2)

(b)

### Cash

| Date | Explanation | Ref. | Debit | Credit | Balance |
|---|---|---|---|---|---|
| Apr. 1 | Balance | √ | | | 14,000 |
| | | | | | |
| | | | | | |
| | | | | | |
| | | | | | |
| | | | | | |
| | | | | | |
| | | | | | |
| | | | | | |
| | | | | | |
| | | | | | |
| | | | | | |

### Accounts Receivable

| Date | Explanation | Ref. | Debit | Credit | Balance |
|---|---|---|---|---|---|
| | | | | | |
| | | | | | |
| | | | | | |
| | | | | | |
| | | | | | |
| | | | | | |

### Merchandise Inventory

| Date | Explanation | Ref. | Debit | Credit | Balance |
|---|---|---|---|---|---|
| Apr. 1 | Balance | √ | | | 3,000 |
| | | | | | |
| | | | | | |
| | | | | | |
| | | | | | |
| | | | | | |
| | | | | | |
| | | | | | |
| | | | | | |
| | | | | | |
| | | | | | |
| | | | | | |
| | | | | | |
| | | | | | |
| | | | | | |
| | | | | | |

Name                                                                     Problem 5-5A Continued (3)

(b)

### Accounts Payable

| Date | Explanation | Ref. | Debit | Credit | Balance |
|------|-------------|------|-------|--------|---------|
|      |             |      |       |        |         |
|      |             |      |       |        |         |
|      |             |      |       |        |         |
|      |             |      |       |        |         |
|      |             |      |       |        |         |
|      |             |      |       |        |         |
|      |             |      |       |        |         |

### M. Nisson, Capital

| Date   | Explanation | Ref. | Debit | Credit | Balance |
|--------|-------------|------|-------|--------|---------|
| Apr. 1 | Balance     | √    |       |        | 17,000  |
|        |             |      |       |        |         |

### Sales

| Date | Explanation | Ref. | Debit | Credit | Balance |
|------|-------------|------|-------|--------|---------|
|      |             |      |       |        |         |
|      |             |      |       |        |         |
|      |             |      |       |        |         |
|      |             |      |       |        |         |

### Sales Returns and Allowances

| Date | Explanation | Ref. | Debit | Credit | Balance |
|------|-------------|------|-------|--------|---------|
|      |             |      |       |        |         |
|      |             |      |       |        |         |
|      |             |      |       |        |         |

### Cost of Goods Sold

| Date | Explanation | Ref. | Debit | Credit | Balance |
|------|-------------|------|-------|--------|---------|
|      |             |      |       |        |         |
|      |             |      |       |        |         |
|      |             |      |       |        |         |
|      |             |      |       |        |         |
|      |             |      |       |        |         |
|      |             |      |       |        |         |
|      |             |      |       |        |         |

### Freight Out

| Date | Explanation | Ref. | Debit | Credit | Balance |
|------|-------------|------|-------|--------|---------|
|      |             |      |       |        |         |
|      |             |      |       |        |         |
|      |             |      |       |        |         |

**Problem 5-5A Concluded**

(c)

*Taking It Further*

Problem 5-6A

(a)

## General Journal

| Date | Account Titles and Explanation | Debit | Credit |
|------|-------------------------------|-------|--------|
|      |                               |       |        |
|      |                               |       |        |
|      |                               |       |        |
|      |                               |       |        |
|      |                               |       |        |

(b)

(c)

Name _____    Problem 5-6A Concluded

(d)

### General Journal

| Date | Account Titles and Explanation | Debit | Credit |
|------|-------------------------------|-------|--------|
|      |                               |       |        |
|      |                               |       |        |
|      |                               |       |        |
|      |                               |       |        |
|      |                               |       |        |
|      |                               |       |        |
|      |                               |       |        |
|      |                               |       |        |
|      |                               |       |        |
|      |                               |       |        |
|      |                               |       |        |
|      |                               |       |        |
|      |                               |       |        |
|      |                               |       |        |
|      |                               |       |        |
|      |                               |       |        |
|      |                               |       |        |
|      |                               |       |        |
|      |                               |       |        |
|      |                               |       |        |
|      |                               |       |        |
|      |                               |       |        |
|      |                               |       |        |

Income Summary

*Taking It Further*

Name  Problem 5-7A

(a)

## General Journal

| Date | Account Titles and Explanation | Debit | Credit |
|------|-------------------------------|-------|--------|
|      |                               |       |        |

(b)

(b) (Continued)

**Problem 5-7A Concluded**

(c)

### General Journal

| Date | Account Titles and Explanation | Debit | Credit |
|------|--------------------------------|-------|--------|
|      |                                |       |        |

(d)

*Taking It Further*

Problem 5-8A

| (a) | 2008 | 2007 | 2006 |
|---|---|---|---|
| Gross profit margin | | | |
| | | | |
| | | | |
| Profit margin | | | |
| | | | |
| | | | |
| Current ratio | | | |
| | | | |
| | | | |
| | | | |

*Taking It Further*

# General Journal

| Date | Account Titles and Explanation | Debit | Credit |
|------|-------------------------------|-------|--------|
|      |                               |       |        |

**Problem 5-9A Concluded**

*Taking It Further*

# General Journal

| Date | Account Titles and Explanation | Debit | Credit |
|---|---|---|---|
| | | | |

*Problem 5-10A Concluded

| General Journal | | | |
|---|---|---|---|
| Date | Account Titles and Explanation | Debit | Credit |
| | | | |

*Taking It Further*

**Problem 5-11A**

(a) General Journal

| Date | Account Titles and Explanation | Debit | Credit |
|------|-------------------------------|-------|--------|
|      |                               |       |        |

**Problem 5-11A Continued (1)**

(a)

### General Journal

| Date | Account Titles and Explanation | Debit | Credit |
|------|-------------------------------|-------|--------|
|      |                               |       |        |

(b)

### Cash

| Date | Explanation | Ref. | Debit | Credit | Balance |
|---|---|---|---|---|---|
| Apr. 1 | Balance | √ | | | 14,000 |
| | | | | | |
| | | | | | |
| | | | | | |
| | | | | | |
| | | | | | |
| | | | | | |
| | | | | | |
| | | | | | |
| | | | | | |
| | | | | | |
| | | | | | |

### Accounts Receivable

| Date | Explanation | Ref. | Debit | Credit | Balance |
|---|---|---|---|---|---|
| | | | | | |
| | | | | | |
| | | | | | |
| | | | | | |
| | | | | | |

### Merchandise Inventory

| Date | Explanation | Ref. | Debit | Credit | Balance |
|---|---|---|---|---|---|
| Apr. 1 | Balance | √ | | | 3,000 |
| | | | | | |

### Accounts Payable

| Date | Explanation | Ref. | Debit | Credit | Balance |
|---|---|---|---|---|---|
| | | | | | |
| | | | | | |
| | | | | | |
| | | | | | |
| | | | | | |
| | | | | | |
| | | | | | |

### M. Nisson, Capital

| Date | Explanation | Ref. | Debit | Credit | Balance |
|---|---|---|---|---|---|
| Apr. 1 | Balance | √ | | | 17,000 |
| | | | | | |

(b)

Sales

| Date | Explanation | Ref. | Debit | Credit | Balance |
|------|-------------|------|-------|--------|---------|
|      |             |      |       |        |         |
|      |             |      |       |        |         |
|      |             |      |       |        |         |

Sales Returns and Allowances

| Date | Explanation | Ref. | Debit | Credit | Balance |
|------|-------------|------|-------|--------|---------|
|      |             |      |       |        |         |
|      |             |      |       |        |         |
|      |             |      |       |        |         |

Purchases

| Date | Explanation | Ref. | Debit | Credit | Balance |
|------|-------------|------|-------|--------|---------|
|      |             |      |       |        |         |
|      |             |      |       |        |         |
|      |             |      |       |        |         |
|      |             |      |       |        |         |
|      |             |      |       |        |         |

Purchase Discounts

| Date | Explanation | Ref. | Debit | Credit | Balance |
|------|-------------|------|-------|--------|---------|
|      |             |      |       |        |         |
|      |             |      |       |        |         |
|      |             |      |       |        |         |

Purchase Returns and Allowances

| Date | Explanation | Ref. | Debit | Credit | Balance |
|------|-------------|------|-------|--------|---------|
|      |             |      |       |        |         |
|      |             |      |       |        |         |
|      |             |      |       |        |         |

Freight In

| Date | Explanation | Ref. | Debit | Credit | Balance |
|------|-------------|------|-------|--------|---------|
|      |             |      |       |        |         |
|      |             |      |       |        |         |
|      |             |      |       |        |         |

Freight Out

| Date | Explanation | Ref. | Debit | Credit | Balance |
|------|-------------|------|-------|--------|---------|
|      |             |      |       |        |         |
|      |             |      |       |        |         |
|      |             |      |       |        |         |

**(c)**

**Taking It Further**

*Problem 5-12A

(a)
## Bud's Bakery
### Income Statement
### Year Ended November 30, 2011

## Bud's Bakery
### Statement of Owner's Equity
### Year Ended November 30, 2011

(a) (Continued)

Bud's Bakery
Balance Sheet
November 30, 2011

**(b)** General Journal

| Date | Account Titles and Explanation | Debit | Credit |
|------|-------------------------------|-------|--------|
|      |                               |       |        |

(c)

**Inventory**

| Date | Explanation | Ref. | Debit | Credit | Balance |
|------|-------------|------|-------|--------|---------|
| Dec. 1 | Balance | √ | | | 34,360 |
| | | | | | |
| | | | | | |
| | | | | | |
| | | | | | |

**B. Hachey, Capital**

| Date | Explanation | Ref. | Debit | Credit | Balance |
|------|-------------|------|-------|--------|---------|
| Dec. 1 | Balance | √ | | | 104,480 |
| | | | | | |
| | | | | | |
| | | | | | |
| | | | | | |

*Taking It Further*

(a)

(b) General Journal

| Date | Account Titles and Explanation | Debit | Credit |
|---|---|---|---|
| | | | |

**(b) (Continued)**

**General Journal**

| Date | Account Titles and Explanation | Debit | Credit |
|------|-------------------------------|-------|--------|
|      |                               |       |        |

(b) and (d)

### Cash

| Date | Explanation | Ref. | Debit | Credit | Balance |
|---|---|---|---|---|---|
| Jan. 1 | Balance | √ | | | 1,130 |
| | | | | | |
| | | | | | |
| | | | | | |
| | | | | | |
| | | | | | |
| | | | | | |
| | | | | | |
| | | | | | |
| | | | | | |
| | | | | | |
| | | | | | |
| | | | | | |
| | | | | | |
| | | | | | |
| | | | | | |

### Accounts Receivable

| Date | Explanation | Ref. | Debit | Credit | Balance |
|---|---|---|---|---|---|
| Jan. 1 | Balance | √ | | | 875 |
| | | | | | |
| | | | | | |
| | | | | | |
| | | | | | |

### Merchandise Inventory

| Date | Explanation | Ref. | Debit | Credit | Balance |
|---|---|---|---|---|---|
| | | | | | |
| | | | | | |
| | | | | | |
| | | | | | |
| | | | | | |
| | | | | | |
| | | | | | |
| | | | | | |
| | | | | | |
| | | | | | |

### Baking Supplies

| Date | Explanation | Ref. | Debit | Credit | Balance |
|---|---|---|---|---|---|
| Jan. 1 | Balance | √ | | | 450 |
| | | | | | |
| | | | | | |

(b) and (d) (Continued)

### Prepaid Insurance

| Date | Explanation | Ref. | Debit | Credit | Balance |
|---|---|---|---|---|---|
| Jan. 1 | Balance | √ | | | 1,100 |
| | | | | | |
| | | | | | |

### Baking Equipment

| Date | Explanation | Ref. | Debit | Credit | Balance |
|---|---|---|---|---|---|
| Jan. 1 | Balance | √ | | | 1,400 |
| | | | | | |
| | | | | | |

### Accumulated Depreciation - Baking Equipment

| Date | Explanation | Ref. | Debit | Credit | Balance |
|---|---|---|---|---|---|
| Jan. 1 | Balance | √ | | | 78 |
| | | | | | |
| | | | | | |
| | | | | | |

### Accounts Payable

| Date | Explanation | Ref. | Debit | Credit | Balance |
|---|---|---|---|---|---|
| Jan. 1 | Balance | √ | | | 75 |
| | | | | | |
| | | | | | |
| | | | | | |
| | | | | | |
| | | | | | |
| | | | | | |

### Salaries Payable

| Date | Explanation | Ref. | Debit | Credit | Balance |
|---|---|---|---|---|---|
| Jan. 1 | Balance | √ | | | 56 |
| | | | | | |
| | | | | | |
| | | | | | |

### Unearned Revenue

| Date | Explanation | Ref. | Debit | Credit | Balance |
|---|---|---|---|---|---|
| Jan. 1 | Balance | √ | | | 300 |
| | | | | | |
| | | | | | |
| | | | | | |

(b) and (d) (Continued)

### Interest Payable

| Date | Explanation | Ref. | Debit | Credit | Balance |
|---|---|---|---|---|---|
| Jan. 1 | Balance | √ | | | 8 |
| | | | | | |
| | | | | | |
| | | | | | |

### Notes Payable

| Date | Explanation | Ref. | Debit | Credit | Balance |
|---|---|---|---|---|---|
| Jan. 1 | Balance | √ | | | 2,000 |
| | | | | | |
| | | | | | |

### N. Koebel, Capital

| Date | Explanation | Ref. | Debit | Credit | Balance |
|---|---|---|---|---|---|
| Jan. 1 | Balance | √ | | | 2,438 |
| | | | | | |
| | | | | | |

### N. Koebel, Drawings

| Date | Explanation | Ref. | Debit | Credit | Balance |
|---|---|---|---|---|---|
| | | | | | |
| | | | | | |
| | | | | | |

### Sales

| Date | Explanation | Ref. | Debit | Credit | Balance |
|---|---|---|---|---|---|
| | | | | | |
| | | | | | |
| | | | | | |
| | | | | | |

### Cost of Goods Sold

| Date | Explanation | Ref. | Debit | Credit | Balance |
|---|---|---|---|---|---|
| | | | | | |
| | | | | | |
| | | | | | |
| | | | | | |

### Salaries Expense

| Date | Explanation | Ref. | Debit | Credit | Balance |
|---|---|---|---|---|---|
| | | | | | |
| | | | | | |
| | | | | | |

(b) and (d) (Continued)

### Telephone Expense

| Date | Explanation | Ref. | Debit | Credit | Balance |
|------|-------------|------|-------|--------|---------|
|      |             |      |       |        |         |
|      |             |      |       |        |         |

### Depreciation Expense

| Date | Explanation | Ref. | Debit | Credit | Balance |
|------|-------------|------|-------|--------|---------|
|      |             |      |       |        |         |
|      |             |      |       |        |         |

### Insurance Expense

| Date | Explanation | Ref. | Debit | Credit | Balance |
|------|-------------|------|-------|--------|---------|
|      |             |      |       |        |         |
|      |             |      |       |        |         |

### Freight Out

| Date | Explanation | Ref. | Debit | Credit | Balance |
|------|-------------|------|-------|--------|---------|
|      |             |      |       |        |         |
|      |             |      |       |        |         |

### Interest Expense

| Date | Explanation | Ref. | Debit | Credit | Balance |
|------|-------------|------|-------|--------|---------|
|      |             |      |       |        |         |
|      |             |      |       |        |         |

### (d) General Journal

| Date | Account Titles and Explanation | Debit | Credit |
|------|--------------------------------|-------|--------|
|      |                                |       |        |
|      |                                |       |        |
|      |                                |       |        |
|      |                                |       |        |
|      |                                |       |        |
|      |                                |       |        |
|      |                                |       |        |
|      |                                |       |        |
|      |                                |       |        |
|      |                                |       |        |
|      |                                |       |        |
|      |                                |       |        |
|      |                                |       |        |
|      |                                |       |        |
|      |                                |       |        |
|      |                                |       |        |
|      |                                |       |        |
|      |                                |       |        |

(c)

| | Debit | Credit |
|---|---|---|
| | | |

(e)

|  | Debit | Credit |
|---|---|---|
|  |  |  |

(f)

(g)

(h)

(a), (b), (d) and (g)

**Cash**

| Date | Explanation | Ref. | Debit | Credit | Balance |
|---|---|---|---|---|---|
| Aug. 1 | Balance | √ | | | 19,985 |
| | | | | | |
| | | | | | |
| | | | | | |
| | | | | | |
| | | | | | |
| | | | | | |
| | | | | | |
| | | | | | |
| | | | | | |
| | | | | | |
| | | | | | |
| | | | | | |
| | | | | | |
| | | | | | |
| | | | | | |
| | | | | | |
| | | | | | |
| | | | | | |

**Accounts Receivable**

| Date | Explanation | Ref. | Debit | Credit | Balance |
|---|---|---|---|---|---|
| | | | | | |
| | | | | | |
| | | | | | |
| | | | | | |
| | | | | | |

**Inventory**

| Date | Explanation | Ref. | Debit | Credit | Balance |
|---|---|---|---|---|---|
| Aug. 1 | Balance | √ | | | 112,700 |
| | | | | | |
| | | | | | |
| | | | | | |
| | | | | | |
| | | | | | |
| | | | | | |
| | | | | | |
| | | | | | |
| | | | | | |
| | | | | | |
| | | | | | |
| | | | | | |
| | | | | | |
| | | | | | |

Name: Cumulative Coverage Continued (1)

(a), (b), (d) and (g) (Continued)

**Store Supplies**

| Date | Explanation | Ref. | Debit | Credit | Balance |
|------|-------------|------|-------|--------|---------|
|      |             |      |       |        |         |
|      |             |      |       |        |         |
|      |             |      |       |        |         |

**Prepaid Insurance**

| Date | Explanation | Ref. | Debit | Credit | Balance |
|------|-------------|------|-------|--------|---------|
| Aug. 1 | Balance | √ |  |  | 4,140 |
|      |             |      |       |        |         |
|      |             |      |       |        |         |

**Store Equipment**

| Date | Explanation | Ref. | Debit | Credit | Balance |
|------|-------------|------|-------|--------|---------|
| Aug. 1 | Balance | √ |  |  | 53,800 |
|      |             |      |       |        |         |

**Accumulated Depreciation - Store Equipment**

| Date | Explanation | Ref. | Debit | Credit | Balance |
|------|-------------|------|-------|--------|---------|
| Aug. 1 | Balance | √ |  |  | 13,450 |
|      |             |      |       |        |         |
|      |             |      |       |        |         |

**Accounts Payable**

| Date | Explanation | Ref. | Debit | Credit | Balance |
|------|-------------|------|-------|--------|---------|
| Aug. 1 | Balance | √ |  |  | 18,620 |
|      |             |      |       |        |         |
|      |             |      |       |        |         |
|      |             |      |       |        |         |
|      |             |      |       |        |         |
|      |             |      |       |        |         |
|      |             |      |       |        |         |
|      |             |      |       |        |         |
|      |             |      |       |        |         |

**Unearned Sales Revenue**

| Date | Explanation | Ref. | Debit | Credit | Balance |
|------|-------------|------|-------|--------|---------|
| Aug. 1 | Balance | √ |  |  | 4,820 |
|      |             |      |       |        |         |
|      |             |      |       |        |         |
|      |             |      |       |        |         |

*Accounting Principles, 5th Canadian Edition*

(a), (b), (d) and (g) (Continued)

### Notes Payable

| Date | Explanation | Ref. | Debit | Credit | Balance |
|---|---|---|---|---|---|
| Aug. 1 | Balance | √ | | | 36,000 |
| | | | | | |
| | | | | | |
| | | | | | |

### Interest Payable

| Date | Explanation | Ref. | Debit | Credit | Balance |
|---|---|---|---|---|---|
| | | | | | |
| | | | | | |
| | | | | | |
| | | | | | |

### Salaries Payable

| Date | Explanation | Ref. | Debit | Credit | Balance |
|---|---|---|---|---|---|
| | | | | | |
| | | | | | |
| | | | | | |
| | | | | | |

### A. John, Capital

| Date | Explanation | Ref. | Debit | Credit | Balance |
|---|---|---|---|---|---|
| Aug. 1 | Balance | √ | | | 54,650 |
| | | | | | |
| | | | | | |
| | | | | | |

### A. John, Drawings

| Date | Explanation | Ref. | Debit | Credit | Balance |
|---|---|---|---|---|---|
| Aug. 1 | Balance | √ | | | 43,300 |
| | | | | | |
| | | | | | |
| | | | | | |

### Income Summary

| Date | Explanation | Ref. | Debit | Credit | Balance |
|---|---|---|---|---|---|
| | | | | | |
| | | | | | |
| | | | | | |
| | | | | | |
| | | | | | |
| | | | | | |

(a), (b), (d), and (g) (Continued)

### Sales

| Date | Explanation | Ref. | Debit | Credit | Balance |
|---|---|---|---|---|---|
| Aug. 1 | Balance | √ | | | 758,500 |
| | | | | | |
| | | | | | |
| | | | | | |
| | | | | | |

### Sales Returns and Allowances

| Date | Sales Returns and Allowance | Ref. | Debit | Credit | Balance |
|---|---|---|---|---|---|
| Aug. 1 | Balance | √ | | | 11,420 |
| | | | | | |
| | | | | | |
| | | | | | |
| | | | | | |

### Sales Discounts

| Date | Sales Returns and Allowance | Ref. | Debit | Credit | Balance |
|---|---|---|---|---|---|
| | | | | | |
| | | | | | |
| | | | | | |
| | | | | | |

### Rent Revenue

| Date | Explanation | Ref. | Debit | Credit | Balance |
|---|---|---|---|---|---|
| Aug. 1 | Balance | √ | | | 1,200 |
| | | | | | |
| | | | | | |
| | | | | | |
| | | | | | |

### Cost of Goods Sold

| Date | Explanation | Ref. | Debit | Credit | Balance |
|---|---|---|---|---|---|
| Aug. 1 | Balance | √ | | | 520,340 |
| | | | | | |
| | | | | | |
| | | | | | |
| | | | | | |
| | | | | | |
| | | | | | |
| | | | | | |

*Accounting Principles, 5th Canadian Edition*

Name     Cumulative Coverage Continued (4)

(a), (b), (d) and (g) (Continued)

### Salaries Expense

| Date | Explanation | Ref. | Debit | Credit | Balance |
|---|---|---|---|---|---|
| Aug. 1 | Balance | √ | | | 92,900 |
| | | | | | |
| | | | | | |
| | | | | | |

### Advertising Expense

| Date | Explanation | Ref. | Debit | Credit | Balance |
|---|---|---|---|---|---|
| Aug. 1 | Balance | √ | | | 9,625 |
| | | | | | |
| | | | | | |
| | | | | | |

### Rent Expense

| Date | Explanation | Ref. | Debit | Credit | Balance |
|---|---|---|---|---|---|
| Aug. 1 | Balance | √ | | | 17,050 |
| | | | | | |
| | | | | | |
| | | | | | |

### Interest Expense

| Date | Sales Returns and Allowance | Ref. | Debit | Credit | Balance |
|---|---|---|---|---|---|
| Aug. 1 | Balance | √ | | | 1,980 |
| | | | | | |
| | | | | | |
| | | | | | |

### Insurance Expense

| Date | Explanation | Ref. | Debit | Credit | Balance |
|---|---|---|---|---|---|
| | | | | | |
| | | | | | |
| | | | | | |
| | | | | | |

### Depreciation Expense

| Date | Explanation | Ref. | Debit | Credit | Balance |
|---|---|---|---|---|---|
| | | | | | |
| | | | | | |
| | | | | | |
| | | | | | |

*Accounting Principles, 5th Canadian Edition*

**(b)** General Journal

| Date | Account Titles and Explanation | Debit | Credit |
|------|-------------------------------|-------|--------|
|      |                               |       |        |

## (b) (Continued) General Journal

| Date | Account Titles and Explanation | Debit | Credit |
|------|-------------------------------|-------|--------|
|      |                               |       |        |

(c)

| | Debit | Credit |
|---|---|---|
| | | |

(d)

## General Journal

| Date | Account Titles and Explanation | Debit | Credit |
|------|-------------------------------|-------|--------|
|      |                               |       |        |

(e)

|  | Debit | Credit |
|---|---|---|
|  |  |  |

(f)

(f) (Continued)

(g)

## General Journal

| Date | Account Titles and Explanation | Debit | Credit |
|------|-------------------------------|-------|--------|
|      |                               |       |        |

(h)

|  | Debit | Credit |
|---|---|---|
|  |  |  |

Name                                                                                                                    Brief Exercises 6-1 to 6-2

**BE6-1**

**BE6-2**

Name

Brief Exercises 6-3 to 6-4

**BE6-3**

| Date | Purchases | | | Cost of Goods Sold | | | Balance | | |
|---|---|---|---|---|---|---|---|---|---|
| | Units | Cost | Total | Units | Cost | Total | Units | Cost | Total |
| Jan. 3 | 3 | $ 1,000.00 | | | | | | | |
| ?? | | | | 1 | | | | | |
| 20 | 2 | $ 1,200.00 | | | | | | | |
| ?? | | | | 1 | | | | | |
| Total | | | | | | | | | |

**BE6-4**

Name _____   Brief Exercises 6-5 to 6-6

**BE6-5**

| Date | Purchases | | | Cost of Goods Sold | | | Balance | | |
| --- | --- | --- | --- | --- | --- | --- | --- | --- | --- |
| | Units | Cost | Total | Units | Cost | Total | Units | Cost | Total |
| June 1 | | | | | | | 200 | $6.00 | $1,200.00 |
| 7 | 400 | $7.35 | $2,940.00 | | | | (a) | (b) | (c) |
| 18 | | | | 350 | (d) | (e) | (f) | (g) | (h) |
| 26 | 375 | $7.90 | 2,962.50 | | | | (i) | (j) | (k) |

**BE6-6**

| Date | Purchases | | | Cost of Goods Sold | | | Balance | | |
| --- | --- | --- | --- | --- | --- | --- | --- | --- | --- |
| | Units | Cost | Total | Units | Cost | Total | Units | Cost | Total |
| June 1 | | | | | | | 200 | $6.00 | $1,200.00 |
| 7 | 400 | $7.35 | $2,940.00 | | | | (a) | (b) | (c) |
| 18 | | | | 350 | (d) | (e) | (f) | (g) | (h) |
| 26 | 375 | $7.90 | 2,962.50 | | | | (i) | (j) | (k) |

Brief Exercise 6-7

(a) FIFO

| Date | Purchases | | | Cost of Goods Sold | | | Balance | | |
|---|---|---|---|---|---|---|---|---|---|
| | Units | Cost | Total | Units | Cost | Total | Units | Cost | Total |
| | | | | | | | | | |
| | | | | | | | | | |
| | | | | | | | | | |
| | | | | | | | | | |
| | | | | | | | | | |
| | | | | | | | | | |
| | | | | | | | | | |
| | | | | | | | | | |
| | | | | | | | | | |
| | | | | | | | | | |
| | | | | | | | | | |
| | | | | | | | | | |
| | | | | | | | | | |
| | | | | | | | | | |
| | | | | | | | | | |

(b) Average

| Date | Purchases | | | Cost of Goods Sold | | | Balance | | |
|---|---|---|---|---|---|---|---|---|---|
| | Units | Cost | Total | Units | Cost | Total | Units | Cost | Total |
| | | | | | | | | | |
| | | | | | | | | | |
| | | | | | | | | | |
| | | | | | | | | | |
| | | | | | | | | | |
| | | | | | | | | | |
| | | | | | | | | | |
| | | | | | | | | | |
| | | | | | | | | | |
| | | | | | | | | | |
| | | | | | | | | | |
| | | | | | | | | | |
| | | | | | | | | | |

**BE6-8**

**BE6-9**

# Brief Exercise 6-10

**BE6-10**

Summary:

| | Assets | = | Liabilities | + | Owner's Equity |
|---|---|---|---|---|---|
| 2010 | | | | | |
| 2011 | | | | | |

Calculations:

Brief Exercise 6-11

## BE6-12

(a)

| Inventory Categories | Cost | NRV | LCNRV |
|---|---|---|---|
| Cameras | 12,000 | 11,200 | |
| Cell phones | 9,000 | 9,500 | |
| DVD players | 14,000 | 10,600 | |
| Total | | | |

(b)

| | Debit | Credit |
|---|---|---|
| | | |
| | | |
| | | |
| | | |

## BE6-13

| Inventory Categories | Cost | NRV | LCNRV |
|---|---|---|---|
| Cameras | 12,000 | 11,200 | |
| Cell phones | 9,000 | 9,500 | |
| Total | | | |

(a)

(b)

Name Exercise 6-5 Concluded

**(b)**

### General Journal

| Date | Account Titles and Explanation | Debit | Credit |
|------|-------------------------------|-------|--------|
|      |                               |       |        |

**(c)**

Name  Exercise 6-6

## (a) (1) FIFO

| Date | Purchases | | | Cost of Goods Sold | | | Balance | | |
|---|---|---|---|---|---|---|---|---|---|
| | Units | Cost | Total | Units | Cost | Total | Units | Cost | Total |
| | | | | | | | | | |
| | | | | | | | | | |
| | | | | | | | | | |
| | | | | | | | | | |
| | | | | | | | | | |
| | | | | | | | | | |
| | | | | | | | | | |
| | | | | | | | | | |
| | | | | | | | | | |
| | | | | | | | | | |
| | | | | | | | | | |
| | | | | | | | | | |
| | | | | | | | | | |
| | | | | | | | | | |
| | | | | | | | | | |
| | | | | | | | | | |
| | | | | | | | | | |
| | | | | | | | | | |
| | | | | | | | | | |
| | | | | | | | | | |
| | | | | | | | | | |
| | | | | | | | | | |

## (2) Average

| Date | Purchases | | | Cost of Goods Sold | | | Balance | | |
|---|---|---|---|---|---|---|---|---|---|
| | Units | Cost | Total | Units | Cost | Total | Units | Cost | Total |
| | | | | | | | | | |
| | | | | | | | | | |
| | | | | | | | | | |
| | | | | | | | | | |
| | | | | | | | | | |
| | | | | | | | | | |
| | | | | | | | | | |
| | | | | | | | | | |
| | | | | | | | | | |
| | | | | | | | | | |
| | | | | | | | | | |
| | | | | | | | | | |
| | | | | | | | | | |
| | | | | | | | | | |
| | | | | | | | | | |
| | | | | | | | | | |
| | | | | | | | | | |

*Accounting Principles, 5th Canadian Edition*  *Working Papers, Chapter*

(b) and (c)

Exercise 6-7

(a)

| | 2011 | 2010 |
|---|---|---|
| | | |

(b)

(c)

Name                                                                                                      Exercise 6-8

(a)

**MARRAKESH COMPANY**
Income Statement (Partial)

| December 31 | 2011 | 2010 |
|---|---|---|
|  |  |  |
|  |  |  |
|  |  |  |
|  |  |  |
|  |  |  |
|  |  |  |
|  |  |  |
|  |  |  |
|  |  |  |
|  |  |  |
|  |  |  |

(b)

(c)

|  | 2011 | 2010 |
|---|---|---|
| Original |  |  |
|  |  |  |
|  |  |  |
|  |  |  |
| Corrected |  |  |
|  |  |  |
|  |  |  |
|  |  |  |

(d)

Name      Exercises 6-9 to 6-10

| E6-9 (a) | Cost | NRV | LCNRV |
|---|---|---|---|
| Cameras | | | |
|   Minolta | | | |
|   Canon | | | |
|     Total | | | |
| Light meters | | | |
|   Vivitar | | | |
|   Kodak | | | |
|     Total | | | |
| Total inventory | | | |

(b) and (c)

| E6-10 | 2008 | 2007 |
|---|---|---|
| Inventory turnover | | |
| Days sales in inventory | | |
| Gross profit margin | | |

*Accounting Principles, 5th Canadian Edition*      *Working Papers, Chapter 6*

Name *Exercise 6-11

| (a) Cost of Goods Available for Sale | Units | Unit Cost | Total Cost |
|---|---|---|---|
| | | | |
| | | | |
| | | | |
| | | | |

**1. FIFO**

**2. Average**

**(b) and (c)**

**Exercise 6-12**

| FIFO |
|---|

| Average |
|---|

Name                                                                                         *Exercise 6-13

### (a) FIFO

| Date | Purchases | | | Cost of Goods Sold | | | Balance | | |
|---|---|---|---|---|---|---|---|---|---|
| | Units | Cost | Total | Units | Cost | Total | Units | Cost | Total |
| | | | | | | | | | |
| | | | | | | | | | |
| | | | | | | | | | |
| | | | | | | | | | |
| | | | | | | | | | |
| | | | | | | | | | |
| | | | | | | | | | |
| | | | | | | | | | |
| | | | | | | | | | |
| | | | | | | | | | |
| | | | | | | | | | |
| | | | | | | | | | |
| | | | | | | | | | |
| | | | | | | | | | |
| | | | | | | | | | |
| | | | | | | | | | |
| | | | | | | | | | |
| | | | | | | | | | |
| | | | | | | | | | |

### Average

| Date | Purchases | | | Cost of Goods Sold | | | Balance | | |
|---|---|---|---|---|---|---|---|---|---|
| | Units | Cost | Total | Units | Cost | Total | Units | Cost | Total |
| | | | | | | | | | |
| | | | | | | | | | |
| | | | | | | | | | |
| | | | | | | | | | |
| | | | | | | | | | |
| | | | | | | | | | |
| | | | | | | | | | |
| | | | | | | | | | |
| | | | | | | | | | |
| | | | | | | | | | |
| | | | | | | | | | |
| | | | | | | | | | |
| | | | | | | | | | |
| | | | | | | | | | |
| | | | | | | | | | |
| | | | | | | | | | |
| | | | | | | | | | |

*Accounting Principles, 5th Canadian Edition*

*Exercise 6-13 Concluded*

(b)

| Cost of Goods Available for Sale | Units | Unit Cost | Total Cost |
|---|---|---|---|
| | | | |
| | | | |
| | | | |
| | | | |
| | | | |
| | | | |
| | | | |

**FIFO**

**Average**

*Exercise 6-14

| Date | General Journal — Account Titles and Explanation | FIFO Dr. | FIFO Cr. | Average Dr. | Average Cr. |
|---|---|---|---|---|---|
| | | | | | |

**E6-15**

| | |
|---|---|
| | |

**E6-16**

| | Men's Shoes | | Women's Shoes | |
|---|---|---|---|---|
| | Cost | Retail | Cost | Retail |
| | | | | |

Name *Exercise 6-17

(a)

| | Running Shoes | | Running Clothes | |
|---|---|---|---|---|
| (b) | Cost | Retail | Cost | Retail |
| | | | | |
| | | | | |
| | | | | |
| | | | | |
| | | | | |
| | | | | |
| | | | | |
| | | | | |
| | | | | |
| | | | | |
| | | | | |
| | | | | |
| | | | | |
| | | | | |

(c)

# Problem 6-4A

**(a)**

| Date | Purchases | | | Cost of Goods Sold | | | Balance | | |
|------|-------|------|-------|-------|------|-------|-------|------|-------|
|  | Units | Cost | Total | Units | Cost | Total | Units | Cost | Total |
|  |  |  |  |  |  |  |  |  |  |
|  |  |  |  |  |  |  |  |  |  |
|  |  |  |  |  |  |  |  |  |  |
|  |  |  |  |  |  |  |  |  |  |

**(b)**

**(c)**

*Taking It Further*

Name _____  Problem 6-5A

**(a) (1) FIFO**

| Date | Purchases | | | Cost of Goods Sold | | | Balance | | |
|---|---|---|---|---|---|---|---|---|---|
| | Units | Cost | Total | Units | Cost | Total | Units | Cost | Total |
| | | | | | | | | | |
| | | | | | | | | | |
| | | | | | | | | | |
| | | | | | | | | | |
| | | | | | | | | | |
| | | | | | | | | | |
| | | | | | | | | | |
| | | | | | | | | | |
| | | | | | | | | | |
| | | | | | | | | | |
| | | | | | | | | | |
| | | | | | | | | | |
| | | | | | | | | | |
| | | | | | | | | | |

**(2) Average**

| Date | Purchases | | | Cost of Goods Sold | | | Balance | | |
|---|---|---|---|---|---|---|---|---|---|
| | Units | Cost | Total | Units | Cost | Total | Units | Cost | Total |
| | | | | | | | | | |
| | | | | | | | | | |
| | | | | | | | | | |
| | | | | | | | | | |
| | | | | | | | | | |
| | | | | | | | | | |
| | | | | | | | | | |
| | | | | | | | | | |
| | | | | | | | | | |

**(b)**

| | FIFO | Average |
|---|---|---|
| | | |
| | | |

**(c)**

*Taking It Further*

Accounting Principles, 5th Canadian Edition                    Working Papers, Chapter

**Problem 6-6A**

| (Optional) | Purchases | | | Cost of Goods Sold | | | Balance | | |
|---|---|---|---|---|---|---|---|---|---|
| Date | Units | Cost | Total | Units | Cost | Total | Units | Cost | Total |
|  |  |  |  |  |  |  |  |  |  |
|  |  |  |  |  |  |  |  |  |  |
|  |  |  |  |  |  |  |  |  |  |
|  |  |  |  |  |  |  |  |  |  |
|  |  |  |  |  |  |  |  |  |  |
|  |  |  |  |  |  |  |  |  |  |
|  |  |  |  |  |  |  |  |  |  |
|  |  |  |  |  |  |  |  |  |  |
|  |  |  |  |  |  |  |  |  |  |
|  |  |  |  |  |  |  |  |  |  |

**(a) General Journal**

| Date | Account Titles and Explanation | Debit | Credit |
|---|---|---|---|
|  |  |  |  |
|  |  |  |  |
|  |  |  |  |
|  |  |  |  |
|  |  |  |  |
|  |  |  |  |
|  |  |  |  |
|  |  |  |  |
|  |  |  |  |
|  |  |  |  |
|  |  |  |  |
|  |  |  |  |
|  |  |  |  |
|  |  |  |  |
|  |  |  |  |
|  |  |  |  |
|  |  |  |  |
|  |  |  |  |
|  |  |  |  |
|  |  |  |  |
|  |  |  |  |
|  |  |  |  |
|  |  |  |  |
|  |  |  |  |
|  |  |  |  |
|  |  |  |  |
|  |  |  |  |
|  |  |  |  |
|  |  |  |  |
|  |  |  |  |
|  |  |  |  |
|  |  |  |  |

*Accounting Principles, 5th Canadian Edition*

**Problem 6-6A Concluded**

(b), (c), and (d)

*Taking It Further*

Name  Problem 6-7A

## (a)

### December-31-09

| | Total Assets | Owner's Equity | Cost of Goods Sold | Profit |
|---|---|---|---|---|
| As reported | $850,000 | $650,000 | $500,000 | $70,000 |
| Impact of Dec. 31, 2009 inventory error | | | | |
| Correct amount | | | | |

### December 31, 2010

| | Total Assets | Owner's Equity | Cost of Goods Sold | Profit |
|---|---|---|---|---|
| As reported | $900,000 | $700,000 | $550,000 | $80,000 |
| Impact of Dec. 31, 2009 inventory error | | | | |
| Impact of Dec. 31, 2010 inventory error | | | | |
| Correct amount | | | | |

### December-31-11

| | Total Assets | Owner's Equity | Cost of Goods Sold | Profit |
|---|---|---|---|---|
| As reported | $925,000 | $750,000 | $550,000 | $90,000 |
| Impact of Dec. 31, 2010 inventory error | | | | |
| Correct amount | | | | |

## (b)

## Taking It Further

*Accounting Principles, 5th Canadian Edition*  *Working Papers, Chapter 6*

Name _____                                          Problem 6-8A

**(a) (Incorrect)**

|  | 2011 | 2010 | 2009 |
|---|---|---|---|
|  |  |  |  |
|  |  |  |  |
|  |  |  |  |
|  |  |  |  |
|  |  |  |  |
|  |  |  |  |

**(Correct)**

|  | 2011 | 2010 | 2009 |
|---|---|---|---|
|  |  |  |  |
|  |  |  |  |
|  |  |  |  |
|  |  |  |  |
|  |  |  |  |
|  |  |  |  |

**(b) and (c)**

*Taking It Further*

*Accounting Principles, 5th Canadian Edition*                                  Working Papers, Chapter

Name                                                                                           Problem 6-9A

(a)
| Date | Tonnes | Total Cost | Total NRV | LCNRV |
|---|---|---|---|---|
| Mar-31 | 3,000 | | | |
| Apr-30 | 2,500 | | | |
| | | | | |
| | | | | |

(b)
| | Debit | Credit |
|---|---|---|
| | | |
| | | |
| | | |
| | | |
| | | |

(c)

(d)

*Taking It Further*

*Accounting Principles, 5th Canadian Edition*                                   *Working Papers, Chapter 6*

Name																																					Problem 6-10A

| PepsiCo Inc. | 2008 | 2007 |
|---|---|---|
| Inventory turnover | | |
| Days sales in inventory | | |
| Current ratio | | |
| Acid-test ratio | | |
| Gross profit margin | | |
| Profit margin | | |

| Coca-Cola Company | 2008 | 2007 |
|---|---|---|
| Inventory turnover | | |
| Days sales in inventory | | |
| Current ratio | | |
| Acid-test ratio | | |
| Gross profit margin | | |
| Profit margin | | |

Accounting Principles, 5th Canadian Edition																																					Working Papers, Chapter

*Taking It Further*

Name *Problem 6-11A

### (a) Cost of Goods Available for Sale

| Date | | Units | Unit Cost | Total Cost |
|---|---|---|---|---|
| | | | | |
| | | | | |
| | | | | |
| | | | | |
| | | | | |
| | | | | |
| | | | | |

### (b) (1) FIFO

### (b) (2) Average

### (c)

### Taking It Further

*Accounting Principles, 5th Canadian Edition*

Name                                                                 *Problem 6-12A

| (a)(1) FIFO-Periodic | | | | |
|---|---|---|---|---|
| Cost of Goods Available for Sale | | | | |
| Date | | Units | Unit Cost | Total Cost |
| | | | | |
| | | | | |
| | | | | |
| | | | | |
| | | | | |
| | | | | |
| | | | | |
| | | | | |
| | | | | |
| | | | | |
| | | | | |
| | | | | |
| | | | | |
| | | | | |
| | | | | |

Name _____  *Problem 6-12A Concluded

### (a) (2) FIFO-Perpetual

| Date | Purchases | | | Cost of Goods Sold | | | Balance | | |
|---|---|---|---|---|---|---|---|---|---|
| | Units | Cost | Total | Units | Cost | Total | Units | Cost | Total |
| | | | | | | | | | |
| | | | | | | | | | |
| | | | | | | | | | |
| | | | | | | | | | |
| | | | | | | | | | |
| | | | | | | | | | |
| | | | | | | | | | |
| | | | | | | | | | |
| | | | | | | | | | |
| | | | | | | | | | |
| | | | | | | | | | |
| | | | | | | | | | |
| | | | | | | | | | |
| | | | | | | | | | |
| | | | | | | | | | |

### (b) Comparison

| | Perpetual | | Periodic | |
|---|---|---|---|---|
| | Ending Inventory | Cost of Goods Sold | Ending Inventory | Cost of Goods Sold |
| | | | | |
| | | | | |
| | | | | |

### Taking It Further

*Problem 6-13A

**(a) Average-Periodic**

Cost of Goods Available for Sale

| Date | | Units | Unit Cost | Total Cost |
|---|---|---|---|---|
| | | | | |
| | | | | |
| | | | | |
| | | | | |
| | | | | |
| | | | | |
| | | | | |

**(2) Average-Perpetual**

| | Purchases | | | Cost of Goods Sold | | | Balance | | |
|---|---|---|---|---|---|---|---|---|---|
| Date | Units | Cost | Total | Units | Cost | Total | Units | Cost | Total |
| | | | | | | | | | |
| | | | | | | | | | |
| | | | | | | | | | |
| | | | | | | | | | |
| | | | | | | | | | |
| | | | | | | | | | |
| | | | | | | | | | |
| | | | | | | | | | |

*Problem 6-13A Concluded

| (b) Comparison | Periodic | | Perpetual | |
|---|---|---|---|---|
| | Ending Inventory | Cost of Goods Sold | Ending Inventory | Cost of Goods Sold |
| | | | | |
| | | | | |
| | | | | |
| | | | | |
| | | | | |

*Taking It Further*

*Problem 6-14A*

Taking It Further

*Problem 6-15A

(a)

| | Video Games | | DVD's | |
|---|---|---|---|---|
| | Cost | Retail | Cost | Retail |
| | | | | |
| | | | | |
| | | | | |
| | | | | |
| | | | | |
| | | | | |
| | | | | |
| | | | | |
| | | | | |
| | | | | |
| | | | | |

Taking It Further

**(a)**

**(b) Average - Perpetual**

| Date | Purchases | | | Cost of Goods Sold | | | Balance | | |
|---|---|---|---|---|---|---|---|---|---|
| | Units | Cost | Total | Units | Cost | Total | Units | Cost | Total |
| | | | | | | | | | |
| | | | | | | | | | |
| | | | | | | | | | |
| | | | | | | | | | |
| | | | | | | | | | |
| | | | | | | | | | |
| | | | | | | | | | |
| | | | | | | | | | |
| | | | | | | | | | |
| | | | | | | | | | |
| | | | | | | | | | |
| | | | | | | | | | |

## (c) and (d)

### General Journal

| Date | Account Titles and Explanation | Debit | Credit |
|------|-------------------------------|-------|--------|
|      |                               |       |        |

Name _____    Brief Exercises 7-1 to 7-4

**BE7-1**

**BE7-2**

**BE7-3** General Journal

| Date | Account Titles and Explanation | Debit | Credit |
|------|-------------------------------|-------|--------|
|      |                               |       |        |
|      |                               |       |        |
|      |                               |       |        |
|      |                               |       |        |
|      |                               |       |        |
|      |                               |       |        |
|      |                               |       |        |
|      |                               |       |        |
|      |                               |       |        |
|      |                               |       |        |
|      |                               |       |        |

**BE7-4**

**Brief Exercises 7-5 to 7-7**

**BE7-5**

### General Journal

| Date | Account Titles and Explanation | Debit | Credit |
|------|-------------------------------|-------|--------|
|      |                               |       |        |
|      |                               |       |        |
|      |                               |       |        |

**BE7-6**

### General Journal

| Date | Account Titles and Explanation | Debit | Credit |
|------|-------------------------------|-------|--------|
|      |                               |       |        |
|      |                               |       |        |
|      |                               |       |        |
|      |                               |       |        |
|      |                               |       |        |

**BE7-7**

| BE7-8 | |
|---|---|
| | 1. EFT payment made by a customer |
| | 2. Bank debit memorandum for service charges |
| | 3. Outstanding cheques from the current month |
| | 4. Bank error in recording a $1,676 deposit as $1,766 |
| | 5. Outstanding cheques from the previous month that are still outstanding |
| | 6. Outstanding cheques from the previous month that are no longer outstanding |
| | 7. Bank error in recording a company cheque made out for $160 as $610 |
| | 8. Bank credit memorandum for interest revenue |
| | 9. Company error in recording a deposit of $1,140 as $1,410 |
| | 10. Bank debit memorandum for an NSF cheque |
| | 11. Deposit in transit from the current month |
| | 12. Company error in recording cheque made out for $450 as $540 |

BE7-9 (a)

(b)

**BE7-10**

**BE7-11**

HOWEL COMPANY
Bank Reconciliation
August 31

Name                                                                 Brief Exercises 7-12 to 7-14

**BE7-12**

General Journal

| Date | Account Titles and Explanation | Debit | Credit |
|---|---|---|---|
| | | | |
| | | | |
| | | | |
| | | | |
| | | | |
| | | | |
| | | | |
| | | | |
| | | | |

**BE7-13**

**BE7-14**

Exercise 7-1

| (a) Component of effective internal control framework | (b) How component contributes to improved internal control |
|---|---|
| | |

Name Exercise 7-2

Exercise 7-3

| (a) Strength or Weakness | (b) Suggested Improvements |
|---|---|
| | |

| (a) Weakness | (b) Suggested Improvements |
| --- | --- |
| | |

# General Journal

| Date | Account Titles and Explanation | Debit | Credit |
|------|-------------------------------|-------|--------|
|      |                               |       |        |

Exercise 7-7

| Date | Account Titles and Explanation | Debit | Credit |
|------|-------------------------------|-------|--------|
|      |                               |       |        |

Name            Exercise 7-8

(a)

(b)

| Date | General Journal — Account Titles and Explanation | Debit | Credit |
|---|---|---|---|
| | | | |

**E7-9**

**E7-10**

Exercise 7-13

(a)

(b)

Problem 7-1A

*Taking It Further*

Name _____   Problem 7-2A

| Internal Control Activities | Application to Cash Receipts |
|---|---|
| | |

**Taking It Further**

# Problem 7-3A

| (a) Weaknesses | (b) Problems |
|---|---|
| | |

*Taking It Further*

**Problem 7-4A**

(a)

### General Journal

| Date | Account Titles and Explanation | Debit | Credit |
|------|-------------------------------|-------|--------|
|      |                               |       |        |

(b)

*Taking It Further*

Name  Problem 7-5A

(a)

(b) and (c)  General Journal

| Date | Account Titles and Explanation | Debit | Credit |
|---|---|---|---|
| | | | |

(d)

**Taking It Further**

(a)

**Problem 7-6A Concluded**

(b)

## General Journal

| Date | Account Titles and Explanation | Debit | Credit |
|------|-------------------------------|-------|--------|
|      |                               |       |        |

*Taking It Further*

**Problem 7-7A**

(a)

(b)

**Problem 7-7A Concluded**

(c)

### General Journal

| Date | Account Titles and Explanation | Debit | Credit |
|------|-------------------------------|-------|--------|
|      |                               |       |        |

*Taking It Further*

Problem 7-8A

(a)

(b)

**Problem 7-8A Concluded**

(c)

### General Journal

| Date | Account Titles and Explanation | Debit | Credit |
|------|-------------------------------|-------|--------|
|      |                               |       |        |

*Taking It Further*

Problem 7-9A

(a)

(b)

Name                                                                 Problem 7-9A Concluded

**(c)**

### General Journal

| Date | Account Titles and Explanation | Debit | Credit |
|------|-------------------------------|-------|--------|
|      |                               |       |        |
|      |                               |       |        |
|      |                               |       |        |
|      |                               |       |        |
|      |                               |       |        |
|      |                               |       |        |
|      |                               |       |        |
|      |                               |       |        |
|      |                               |       |        |
|      |                               |       |        |
|      |                               |       |        |
|      |                               |       |        |
|      |                               |       |        |

**(d)**

*Taking It Further*

*Accounting Principles, 5th Canadian Edition*                                       Working Papers, Chapter

(a)

(b)

*Taking It Further*

Problem 7-11A

(a)

(b)

Taking It Further

# Continuing Cookie Chronicle

(a)

| Weakness | Control Activity Violated |
|---|---|
| | |

(b) and (c)

Name:

Name

| Date | General Journal<br>Account Titles and Explanation | Debit | Credit |
|---|---|---|---|
| | | | |

Name:

Accounting Principles, 5th Canadian Edition                    Working Papers, Blank Forms

Name:

| Date | Explanation | Ref. | Debit | Credit | Balance |
|------|-------------|------|-------|--------|---------|
|      |             |      |       |        |         |
|      |             |      |       |        |         |
|      |             |      |       |        |         |
|      |             |      |       |        |         |
|      |             |      |       |        |         |
|      |             |      |       |        |         |
|      |             |      |       |        |         |
|      |             |      |       |        |         |
|      |             |      |       |        |         |
|      |             |      |       |        |         |
|      |             |      |       |        |         |
|      |             |      |       |        |         |

| Date | Explanation | Ref. | Debit | Credit | Balance |
|------|-------------|------|-------|--------|---------|
|      |             |      |       |        |         |
|      |             |      |       |        |         |
|      |             |      |       |        |         |
|      |             |      |       |        |         |
|      |             |      |       |        |         |
|      |             |      |       |        |         |
|      |             |      |       |        |         |
|      |             |      |       |        |         |
|      |             |      |       |        |         |
|      |             |      |       |        |         |

| Date | Explanation | Ref. | Debit | Credit | Balance |
|------|-------------|------|-------|--------|---------|
|      |             |      |       |        |         |
|      |             |      |       |        |         |
|      |             |      |       |        |         |
|      |             |      |       |        |         |
|      |             |      |       |        |         |

| Date | Explanation | Ref. | Debit | Credit | Balance |
|------|-------------|------|-------|--------|---------|
|      |             |      |       |        |         |
|      |             |      |       |        |         |
|      |             |      |       |        |         |
|      |             |      |       |        |         |
|      |             |      |       |        |         |

*Accounting Principles, 5th Canadian Edition*  *Working Papers, Blank Form*

Name:

|  | Debit | Credit |
|---|---|---|
|  |  |  |

Name

*Accounting Principles, 5th Canadian Edition* — *Working Papers, Blank Form*

*Taking It Further*